Lighthouse

Women Leading the Way in Finance

Dedicated to my lighthouses

CONTENTS

FOREWORD   **I**

INTRODUCTION   **- 1 -**

FOUNDERS   **- 11 -**

PERTH TOLLE   - 13 -
LAUREN TEMPLETON   - 19 -
MARGARET RUST   - 25 -
FRAN SKINNER   - 33 -
SONYA DREIZLER   - 39 -
VICKI SAUNDERS   - 45 -

LEADERS   **- 51 -**

HEATHER BRILLIANT   - 53 -
DENISE STRACK   - 61 -
LISA SHALETT   - 65 -
CALLIE HAINES   - 77 -
LISA TEPPER   - 81 -

MANAGERS AND ANALYSTS   **- 87 -**

KATHERINE FISCHER   - 89 -
ERIN LASH   - 95 -
JENN COLE   - 103 -
JEN LIKANDER   - 109 -

CHAMPIONS OF SOCIALLY RESPONSIBLE INVESTING   **- 115 -**

ALYCE LOMAX   - 117 -
SHILPA ANDALKAR   - 123 -

STUDENTS — 127 —

    MONSOON PABRAI — 129 —
    MICHELLE SINDHUNIRMALA — 135 —

MY STORY — 139 —

APPENDIX A — 151 —

APPENDIX B — 156 —

GLOSSARY — 157 —

SOURCES — 158 —

Foreword

When seventeen-year-old Maya Peterson asked me to write the foreword for her book, *Lighthouse: Women Leading the Way in Finance*, I was in awe. Few of us are organized enough at the tender age of seventeen to do anything noteworthy, let alone be the author of two published books. Peterson's first was *Early Bird: The Power of Investing Young*, published when she was fourteen.

Throughout our discussion, it is apparent to me that Peterson has an incredibly clear vision of what she wants to accomplish with the book and a plan to get there. She does not waver from that. Again, a remarkable feat for a seventeen-year-old. But what astonished me the most was that Peterson, at this young age, has the maturity to realize that youth who seek inspiration need a lighthouse figure, much like the women leaders featured in her book. This shows maturity and understanding beyond her age, but at the same time, conveys her incredible humility.

A lighthouse provides navigational guidance to boats. In turbulent waters, it can be the critical survival tool that a weary traveler needs. A lighthouse figure in life shows us that it is possible to break out of the mundane and rise up from adversity. Without that, some of us may never fully realize our potential or find our way to clarity.

I am a venture capitalist who came to this role via an unlikely path. From an immigrant who arrived in the USA with nothing to my name to founding my own venture investment firm, I know the impact of lighthouse figures only too well. Starting with my mother, who went against her family's wishes to pursue higher education, to the many mentors and friends who helped and guided me, those role models had a critical impact on my life and career. Having such a lighthouse in one's life, I believe, is an issue of absolute necessity.

That said, this book, *Lighthouse: Women Leading the Way in Finance*, is not just about the success of women leaders; it is also a collection of remarkable human-interest stories. In her writing, Peterson focused on the human and the women's own lighthouses behind their success—the grandmother who inspired, the math teacher who brought to light a whole new world—and delivered a wonderful tale of human resilience and growth.

We can all use a lighthouse in our lives. I have no doubt that Peterson and her book will be one of the bright ones.

—Dr. Chenxi Wang, Founder and General Partner at Rain Capital

Introduction

Lighthouses guide boats at sea and stand proudly as a reminder of strength, comfort, and safe passage. They keep travelers safe from rocks, blinding fog, and dangerous storms. This book is a compilation of stories from female lighthouses in the world of finance: their stories, their struggles, their success, and what drives them. These women's experiences vary tremendously, which provides readers with a wide choice of light to illuminate their own path in life.

I wrote this book to inspire and empower women to persist through challenges in their careers, as my lighthouses have inspired me. The women in this book pushed through a lot of obstacles to get where they are today. One mailed thousands of resumes to potential companies to be offered just one interview; a handful went into their career with a clear vision of what they wanted to do and did it; others tried to avoid finance altogether; and one was preoccupied with being part of the US Olympic gymnastics team, but all of them have persisted through struggles in their career. Their individual struggles, from becoming workaholics to handling the ongoing sexist *noise* to balancing work and family life is not what they have in common. What they all have in common is that they found ways to overcome their individual challenges. I hope their stories inspire you as much as they did me.

I wrote my first book, *Early Bird: The Power of Investing Young,* when I was thirteen. Three years later, it was included in the curriculum for young people at both high schools and colleges. It has helped new investors get started. Helping young people start investing is a passion of mine because they have the most time. In the fall of 2018, I was invited to the University of Massachusetts Isenberg School of Management to speak to the Women and Securities group, who used my book as a basis for a group study project. Forty-five students in their early twenties, mostly women, went around the table introducing themselves and asking me questions or commenting on my book about investing, my journey, and more. One student's comment stood out from all of the rest and inspired me to write this book, despite the fact that I was a junior in high school with an already very full plate. She called me "a lighthouse for young women in finance." Her comment stuck with me. Here I was in a room full of young women who were reading my first book because that book was the only one written for young people by a young woman. That is when I knew I had to do more. Lighthouse was born.

Throughout my life, I have been surrounded by lighthouses, from my great grandmother who ran a hotel in the 1950s, years before most women ran businesses, to my mother and father who are both entrepreneurs. I entered the finance community without knowing what to expect, but I was surprised by how many professionals respected and invested in me as a young person. No one has believed in or encouraged me as much as my parents. My father continues to be one of my biggest inspirations. In any time of hardship, I know I will have my dad to turn to, and he will congratulate me that I made my one mistake for the day. Thanks to my mother's curiosity and desire to learn, I have learned to push myself to my greatest potential. My brother, who was the first person to get his hands on *Early Bird,* will always be my number-one supporter. He will help me with whatever I need whenever I need help;

he will talk with me about anything from his science fair project to The Home Depot's sales. I also want to thank my grandfather for selling my books to his harbormaster, his barber, and anyone unfortunate enough to stand in front of him in line at the grocery store.

My list of lighthouses is long and includes some you will have the pleasure of reading about in this book. The list starts with Todd Wenning, a generous and supportive mentor and friend who showed me respect when I was very young. Erin Lash always answers my emails bombarding her with questions about her career, her life, and her writing. Adrian Lane has always stood by my side as one of my biggest supporters. Jim Ross featured my book at Berkshire Hathaway. Hope Nelson-Pope taught me that writing is mostly editing, and she worked tirelessly on perfecting my first blog post. LouAnn Lofton's book, *Warren Buffett Invests Like a Girl: And Why You Should Too,* inspired me to invest like a girl confidently. Patrick and Robert Gaughen shared their story of how they built Hingham. Alyce Lomax opened my eyes to socially responsible investing before it was the thing to do. David Gardner invited me to coffee at the "Women Investing Foolishly" program when I was ten and graciously gave me an interview for my first book. Sean Stannard-Stockton gave me a platform to speak about my journey and my book. Warren Buffett sent me a note congratulating me on my book, as did Charlie Munger. Aunt Ginny showed me the joy of investing and eating cookies at the same time. Farhang Kassaei, Saurabh Madaan, Ashok Talapatra, and Pranesh Srinivasan, members of the Value Investment Club at Google, brought me to Google, not once but twice, to be part of the investing conversation. Bill Mann, David Kretzman, and Jason Moser taught me to Foolishly invest. Growing up, I felt my career options were endless, and that is all thanks to my wonderful lighthouses.

As I have grown older and become more immersed in the finance community, my list of lighthouses has grown exponentially, but the number of female leaders in the finance industry is still limited. I first noticed this in 2013. I was ten years old and ready to start my search for open chief financial officer (CFO) positions. My first step in planning my career was to create a poster board of pictures and extended biographies of all the female CFOs of Fortune 500 companies at that time. Unfortunately, my poster board only consisted of fifty-eight women out of all 500 companies. [1] That horrible percentage did not make me hesitant about continuing my search for female CFOs, because during that time, I met Lauren Templeton.

I was just starting to save my money and learning to invest. My father told me stories about someone named Lauren Templeton. When she was my age, she wallpapered her room with stock certificates. She took her role as a part-owner of a business seriously. Once, she walked into Walmart, one of her holdings, and was so disappointed at the poor state of the bathrooms that she wrote a letter to Sam Walton, the founder. She knew that because she owned Walmart stock, she was a crucial, part-owner in the business. She received a letter from Walton, saying he would make sure the bathroom problem was fixed. After hearing Lauren's stories, I was determined to meet her. Her childhood persistence and passion guided my journey. She became my lighthouse.

In 2013, I attended the Berkshire Hathaway annual shareholders meeting. Of course, I was eager to hear Warren Buffett speak but even more excited by the book signing, right before the meeting. Lauren Templeton would be signing her book, *Investing the Templeton Way*. My first stop was her table, but she wasn't there. Instead, Scott, her husband, greeted me, a beaming ten-year-old, with the disappointing news that Lauren was not there. I later learned that she had just had her second child. He gave me her business card, which sported a sparkly, gold owl in the right corner. The second I got home, I wrote her a letter to tell her how excited I was to learn her story, and I also mentioned that I loved the sparkly owl, which make her business card the coolest one I had ever seen. She sent me a very kind letter in reply and a package that contained signed copies of all of her books. She bookmarked and annotated the parts she thought I would particularly enjoy *and* all of the readings her father gave her when she started to learn about investing. What an amazing gift and surprise it was for me that a woman in her position would light my way and take a ten-year-old seriously. How could that not make me feel invincible even as a *very* young woman in finance?

Meanwhile, I had wallpapered my room with pictures of fifty-eight female CFOs in an attempt to figure out how I could become a CFO. I took thorough notes on their childhood, education, and career paths, hoping to mimic them in my life. Now, seven years later, *Lighthouse* is the newer version of that wallpaper, with a deeper dive through interviews and research. I am still fascinated with women leaders and what it takes for them to succeed. So it shocks me to think that only one in five women have a C-Suite job and fewer than one in thirty are women of color.[2]

I like to think that if women were given a fair, unbiased chance in finance, I would have at least 250 women on my board, not fifty-eight.

As my interest in business grew, I started an investing blog called *Compounding Snowballs*. I wrote about the long-term math of compounding and how to get it to work for young people. After I started my blog, I wrote my first book, *Early Bird: The Power of Investing Young,* and as my network of women in finance grew, I continued to find more lighthouses. Motivated to learn and tell the stories of female leaders in finance, I decided to write this book. Their stories opened my eyes to their real lives, and each interview inspired me and sent me running to share my impressions with my family, and happily back to my computer to write.

Allies and Advocates and What It Takes to be One

There is an old saying: "Behind every successful man, there is a strong woman." The reverse is equally true. Every good leader needs support. A good boss recognizes ability, advocates for people with potential and talent, and promotes people regardless of gender.

Each of our journeys to find a career is different, but we have common goals of being happy, supported, and successful. Optimizing our strengths and understanding our weaknesses moves us toward establishing a comfortable career. However, there are limits to what anyone can do when not supported or validated. Never underestimate the power of support. For example, the CEO of the company Lisa Tepper worked at personally reached out to her and pushed her to take a promotion she felt she did not deserve. Perth Tolle's support system enabled her to start her own exchange traded fund (ETF). Sonya Dreizler also had a CEO who believed in her and was willing to take a chance with her. We all need someone who believes in us enough to push our limits and help us achieve our greatest potential.

Whether support and validation comes from a female advocate or a male ally, it is crucial to a healthy work environment—and any other environment. Male allies are defined as "members of an advantaged group committed to building relationships with women, expressing as little sexism in their own behavior as possible, understanding the social privilege conferred by their gender, and demonstrating active efforts to address gender inequities at work and in society."[3] Allies have the ability to challenge existing, sexist structures within a company without the unnecessarily extreme repercussions that some women might otherwise encounter. While research varies about the downside of being an ally, male allies can be a catalyst for positive change that sets an expectation of how women should be treated: respectfully. Regardless of gender, it is important to feel supported and heard. The women in my book relied on support to help them through difficult times, as well as challenge and push themselves. When it comes to having a family, it is especially important to find an employer who understands the difficulties of balancing family life and work. Throughout the hardships they faced, having an advocate, or having a loved one's support, was crucial. Building a community of "kick-ass" women in finance, as Sonya Dreizler likes to call it, helps tremendously. Supportive networks are incredibly powerful, and they work both ways with others offering support to you and you offering support to others. Seek out your lighthouses, and where you can, serve as a lighthouse for others.

Female Advocates and Mentoring

When Lauren Templeton shared her experience of women working against her, I was shocked, but she was right. I did some digging and found out that female leaders in higher positions who advocate for junior women are more likely to receive a negative performance review from their boss.[4] Consequently, women are less likely to be promoted. "Women, in general, are less likely to give a hand up because they have fought for so long," Lauren told me during our interview. Only a small number of women make it to executive roles, the same women who are juggling child care and pregnancies and fighting their own battles on top of high-stress jobs in the finance world. They don't have a lot of incentive to help junior women, especially at the cost of their own job.

The women I interviewed shared a universal warning about the struggle of balancing a family and a career in graduate school. They had to navigate a whole family full of challenges. In every case, a supportive spouse tilted the scale, but everyone found the balance difficult to maintain. Many women got lost in their work and needed major life changes in order to regain their family balance. Many women are also juggling a heavy load of family responsibilities. Denise Strack pursued her MBA while pregnant and took care of her newborn during her first job out of school. Some of these women had to make the difficult choice of putting their family lives on hold while they furthered their careers, because going back to work after having a child is a struggle. It reportedly takes two and half years before 74 percent of women who left the workforce return, and only 40 percent will return to a full-time job. [5]

Making Change

Women are leading change across the business ecosystem. This shows up in many different ways in the stories you are about to read. One concrete example is putting investing into a broader context, sometimes referred to as environmental, social, and governance (ESG) investing, or socially responsible investing (SRI). About a fifth of the women I interviewed are involved in SRI/ESG in one way or another.

SRI is a good illustration of a specific trend that promotes the concept of making changes on a broader scale. As an investor, when you buy stock in a company, you become a part-owner of that business. Effective long-term investing is about finding companies that will thrive for decades, not weeks. The modern world is very short-term focused. Supposedly, we are in the information age, but daily blips and tweets stir confusion and panic. Can we navigate through the contemporary, short-term-focused world to get to the much longer time horizons that effective investing requires?

British asset management guru, Jeremy Grantham, observed in a speech at Morningstar's 2018 investing conference that "capitalism has a severe problem with the very long term. Anything that happens to a corporation over 25 years out doesn't really matter to them. Therefore, in that logic, grandchildren have no value. We deforest the land, we degrade our soils, we pollute and overuse our water, and we treat our air like an open sewer. All of this is off the balance sheet and off the income statement."[6] Warren Buffett put it eloquently when he observed that "life is like a snowball. The important thing is finding wet snow and a really long hill."[7] Capitalists who believe the only thing that matters is this quarter and this year run a major risk of destroying long-term value and missing opportunities to create value. When business leaders look to the distant horizon, they make decisions with their children and grandchildren in mind.

Find the Center of the Venn

Another thing that stood out to me from my interviews and research is that those women who were not involved in SRI/ESG still were directly or indirectly advocates for change, whether that meant creating a place for young women to hone their innovation, emphasizing and investing in free markets, creating a flatter company, trying to attack environmental issues from a different angle, or finding the best people for the role.

These women had the will to make a change. They came to new ideas and jobs from a place of change and passion, not from a place of greed or wealth. And throughout their careers they were adaptable. Katie Hall founded two firms and Vicki Saunders developed and improved her many global initiatives until she got it right. Most did not know what they wanted to do with their life. They did not have a plan, but with passion and drive they changed the broader landscape by lining up opportunities with their own capabilities, whether the world was ready at first to recognize them or not.

Finding Your Path: How to use this book

The book is divided into five main sections titled Founders, Leaders, Managers and Analysts, SRI Champions, and Students. My research on these women included personal interviews with each professional as well as research conducted online and in print. The interview dates are given in Appendix B, and the endnotes at the back of this book list the other sources I used to create the individual profile of each woman. Descriptions of SRI and ESG are found in Appendix A As every boat that passes a lighthouse is on its own journey, each woman's story in this book is a unique combination of opportunities and challenges and how they met them. Yours will be too. I hope that lighthouses will shine somewhere in your life as they have in mine. And better yet, be one!

Founders

Perth Tolle

Lighthouses in Perth's Words

"We launched the ETF on May 23. And in early June, democracy protests began in Hong Kong. Millions came out to stand up for freedom in their city. It's been five months and they're still fighting out on the streets. No matter what happens, what they are doing is historic. It was in Hong Kong that I first saw the impact freedom made, in my life, in society, and in economies and markets. And it's the Hong Kong protesters that are now risking their lives and futures every day to stand up for freedom. They are my lighthouse, these freedom fighters and others fighting repressive regimes all over the world. I'm building this company, using the tools I have, indexing, to provide an alternative for investors who want to take a stand for freedom with their emerging market allocations."

Early Years

Perth Tolle attended Trinity University in Texas with an unclear idea of what she wanted to study. She studied business because it was what came most naturally, but along the way, she took an interest in more creative fields. The summer before her senior year in college, she went to ArtCenter College of Design in Pasadena to study advertising and graphic design. "There I realized that while I enjoyed design, my talent level as a graphic designer was, let's just say, not up to par with the other students. So, I came back to Trinity and finished my business degree with finance and marketing concentrations."

After graduating cum laude, she moved to Hong Kong for about one year, which is where her real interest in finance and freedom began: "I witnessed things that made me realize how different my life would have been had I not moved to the USA as a child." What stood out to her about China was the lack of freedom in the markets: "It was clear that freedom made a difference in my life and it makes a difference in markets. I also saw the impact of the One Child policy on the culture of my generation, how it changed our mindset, changed the things we value, changed the demographic trends of the country, and realized that policies and governance make a huge impact on the future growth and sustainability of a market and society."

Path to Success

After returning to the USA, Perth started working for Fidelity as a financial advisor in the Texas and California branches, and that is where she really learned about investing. As a financial advisor at Fidelity, she learned how to build a portfolio and understand investor behavior. She understood how emerging markets fit into a diversified portfolio, and she understood firsthand that aligning clients' values with their investments was not always easy to do because money is personal and not always rational. But she also learned that investors can stick to their plans more easily if their investments align with their convictions. She was surrounded by bosses who pushed her to keep learning and colleagues who cared as much about their clients as the market.

After becoming a mom, Perth made the decision to leave Fidelity to stay home with her young daughter until she started school. At that point, Perth began working on her new venture, starting her own index, and later, an exchange traded fund (ETF) based on that index.

Perth wanted to make it simple for investors to participate in emerging markets and also avoid the downsides of some of the negative policies and governance she found in China and other less free markets. Because this combination was not readily available to most investors, who simply bought a market-capitalization-weighted, emerging-markets fund, she started her own index company: Life + Liberty Indexes. If this sounds hard to do, it probably is for most people, but Perth found a way. "What I have learned and continue to learn through this is that when we are called to do something, we will be equipped to do it, even if we have legit excuses not to, such as "I'm a single mom." Don't give yourself any excuses; just do what you know you have a fire inside to do. And if it's truly a calling, you will be equipped to do it. That doesn't mean success is guaranteed, just that you decide the risk is worth it. I realized I would rather fail at this than not try it." One of her "mom friends" came up with the ticker for her first index (FRDM) when she was in the grocery store and texted it to Perth. Another did her website and graphic design. Their mission is to "create strategies that empower investors who believe in freedom to invest in alignment with their values—direct investment allocations to markets that protect and promote human and economic freedoms and provide an alternative to market-capitalization-weighted country allocations in emerging market indexes."

Although Life + Liberty focuses on emerging markets, it does not include the classic BRICs. "We determine country inclusion and weight based on their freedom levels. We isolate the freedom factor on the country level, and we look at just their level of protection for human and economic freedom, and that alone determines if the country is included, and what its allocation is in the index." However, if a country in the index experiences a rapid decline in freedom levels, as Turkey did in 2017, they can be kicked out of the index.

The biggest challenge in the beginning of the project was that there was no comprehensive quantitative measure of human freedom. So, Perth's company developed and provisionally patented a way to quantify freedom using ordinal scales. A couple years later, when she started scoring countries using this system, she found that the Fraser Institute, the Cato Institute, and the Friedrich Naumann Foundation had started to quantify human freedoms in much the same way she did. As a result, she decided to go with their data set for third-party objectivity. Her independence from these think tanks would assure her investors that she could not "game the system to arbitrarily include or exclude any country." These data providers evaluate each country with seventy-nine objectives, quantified freedom variables, encompassing both personal and economic freedoms.[8] Her index fund works to put money into freer, developing countries.

In order to build an index, Perth had to write the index methodology, find an index calculator, and publish the new index. She originally published her index in 2014, using freedom metrics combined with other factors such as valuations and yield. But when she presented her concept of focusing solely on freedom to advisors and portfolio managers, she got lots of feedback along the lines of "If they [investors] wanted to tilt to value, or dividends, they could do that on their own." Sam Rines, a local advisor in Houston, told her, "Look, freedom is the real innovation here." Perth decided to isolate the freedom factor in her index. Life + Liberty Indexes looks at three aspects of freedom: political, civil, and economic (see Fig. 1 below).

Figure 1. Freedom Factors of Life + Liberty Indexes

Freedom:	Political Freedom	Economic Freedom	Civil Freedom
How it is measured:	Rule of law, due process, judicial independence, plurality of political parties, corruption and transparency, freedom of movement, expression, religion, assembly, the press, and association, and Internet freedom.	Size of government, legal system and property rights, sound monetary policy, freedom to trade internationally, business, credit, and labor regulations.	Violent conflict, internal organized crime, terrorism, trafficking, disappearances, detainments, torture, and women's freedoms.

Launching Her ETF

Getting her fund to market was another odyssey. Perth negotiated a lot of deals that fell through, teaching her the importance of having patience and confidence in the concept. Eventually she found the perfect partner in Alpha Architect, a group of US Marines PhDs who are passionate about ETFs and freedom. Before she found Alpha Architect, she almost completed a deal with one of her top issuers, and although it was not the best deal from her perspective, she thought it would give the ETF the best chances of success. Once she agreed to it, the issuer began to hesitate: "I went to Inside ETFs, a big ETF conference in Florida, near Miami. Every year at this conference I give myself a few extra hours at the beach on the last day before heading home. So, on the last day, after I had lunch with Rob Arnott (indexing legend and my first seed investor and future partner in the firm), then sat outside at the bar for a while with Reggie Browne (ETF legend who ended up becoming my lead market maker), I headed toward the beach and checked my emails. There was an email from the CEO of this issuer, backing out of the deal. It was the worst end to any Inside ETFs ever. The next day it was fine, but it was super sad at the time. Still, by then I had gone through enough in this endeavor that I knew things happened for a reason, and I had no doubt that I should keep going. I do want to note that through the experience, all friendships survived and even grew. In the ETF industry, where everyone is an underdog, especially the indie issuers, everyone sticks together and that goes beyond these temporary things like job offers. We'll all still be buddies long after this is all over. And I love that about this industry and the people in it." Her current issuer is ideal for her project.

Philosophy

Perth's work is a good example of value plus value. Her fund opens up new ways for individual US investors (large and small) who believe in the benefits of freedom to participate in fast-growing emerging markets around the world, and to do so while aligning their portfolios with their values.

Lauren Templeton

Lighthouses in Lauren's Words

"There have been several lighthouses in my life. The most important is my father who has always encouraged me to test my ideas and not fear failure. Failure in a calculated risk was acceptable; not trying at all was the real risk. It is a unique mindset. He has always encouraged me to go for it and try it, where experience could either lead to wealth or a tough lesson. Both have value. John Templeton was a lighthouse. I did manage money with him; I did have a relationship with him, but it was in a very condensed period of my life for around ten years. During that time, we had a close relationship. Over that time, I craved his wisdom, writings, faxes, and his lessons on investing. I absorbed as much as I possibly could. Like my father, he did not fear failure. I never saw him show much emotion at all when investing. He constantly tried new ideas and either did remarkably well or learned a valuable lesson. In either case he remained positive and undeterred.

We also have an investor at our firm that I consider a lighthouse. He is a true leader and just an amazing and generous person. He was a professional athlete and the CEO of a publicly traded company. He is very smart and well read. I learn something from him at almost every meeting. Again though, much like my father and Sir John, he has a deeply positive mindset and disposition. His attitude is contagious, and I see it rub off on the people he associates with including his family and business relationships."

Early Years

As a child, Lauren Templeton's bedtime stories occasionally included fairy tales, but it was her father's favorite narrative on the "magic" of compounding that she remembers best. She jokes that while she learned an important concept, she also fell fast asleep. Her father took her on trips to visit the sites of companies where she was invested, such as Walmart, and her bedroom was wallpapered in stock certificates from her monthly investments. From these early experiences she never strayed too far from the world of investing. After graduating from The University of the South in Sewanee, Tennessee, Lauren worked as a junior associate for the financial advisor Homrich Berg. She later worked for a hedge fund management company, New Providence Advisors. In only three years following college graduation, Lauren created her own firm in 2001, Templeton Capital Management (Templeton and Phillips, today), that served as a general partner to a long/short equity hedge fund that she launched. She has been running her firm ever since and has also become an author along the way, coauthoring *Investing the Templeton Way.*

Lauren's uncle, Sir John Templeton, was a famous global value investor whose career rose to stardom during her childhood. Also, when Lauren was still a child, her parents caught the investing bug and sold their businesses—a hardware store and a motorcycle dealership—to return to school to become full-time investors. During those impressionable years, Lauren soaked up from her parents the concepts and terminology that are daunting to many individual investors. From age eight, thoughts and discussions on investing eventually became second nature to her. She found investments fascinating, and her parents indulged her interest. They gave her the freedom to choose her own investments, with the idea that it was the best way for her to learn. Neither parent questioned her decision making or pushed back on her stock selections. As time went on, Lauren's interests naturally shifted towards broader interests in school and outside activities. Although she was smart and never stopped saving and investing, she did not want to spend her free time looking at stocks and instead allocated her ongoing savings to mutual funds. It was not until she attended college that she returned to stock picking.

Path to Success

It was not long after she began her career that Lauren caught the attention of her famous uncle. One day, in late 2000, she received a fax from Sir John that read, "I am seeding a hedge fund for you with $30 million. If you want to have better performance than the crowd, you must do things differently." By starting her own hedge fund at age twenty-four, Lauren found herself far removed from the crowd: "I knew immediately that I had a tremendous opportunity to learn from one of the very best, but do not think for a second that my path has been easy."

From my conversations with Lauren, I have learned that she is confident and determined, but she said something unexpected: "I think women are bad at raising money because few of us have the confidence to go ask for it. I am not good at raising capital. Do you know why? Because I have never asked for any of it. I don't ever ask. Our business has grown organically. That is a wonderful way to grow a business—by referral—but the business could be a lot better if I did what men do. Men slide a presentation across the table and say, 'I want you to invest with me.' Women are more like, 'How can I help you?'"

Throughout her career she learned the art of being unpopular at times, perhaps because she was a woman in investing or because of her investment philosophy: "Looking back on our firm's success, one of the great factors was putting a lot of money to work during the financial crisis when other people weren't," she told me in our interview. While Templeton and Phillips Capital Management invested during the Great Recession lows in March 2009, Lauren was going into labor with her first child. She and her husband, Scott, were actively purchasing stocks on a laptop in the delivery room—doing things differently!

The Importance of Separating Emotions from Investing

Sir John was known for his ability to separate his emotions from investing, thereby enabling his global value investing philosophy to pay off over the long term. Lauren's hedge fund began strictly with US equities that were selected through quantitative methods in order to sidestep the emotional pitfalls that young investors encounter. The fund's philosophy evolved to incorporate the wisdom of her uncle, and she began investing globally. Her success can be credited to her ability to remain calm in hectic moments in the market: "My old office in downtown Chattanooga had the phrase 'Trouble Is Opportunity' in big gold letters above the front door, instead of 'Templeton and Phillips.' If an investor asked, 'What does that phrase mean?' I knew we were a poor match." As the market rose and fell, Lauren understood what it meant to witness the emotional highs and lows while maintaining a steady hand.

Sexism and Intimidation in the Industry

In addition to dealing with the stress of the markets, Lauren dealt with the ageist and sexist tendencies of male brokers. "I have dealt with my fair share of turkeys," she told me. Throughout her time with one of her prime brokers, her relationship was far from pleasant: "Maybe it was because I was a woman, maybe it was because I was a young person, or maybe it was because I was a young woman." For example, early in her career, she had negotiated a favorable debit-credit spread with her prime broker. She had been introduced to the broker through a well-known ex-Templeton manager, so she trusted the company. However, she noticed on her initial custodial report that the prime broker had not applied the negotiated (and contracted) rates for her account, thereby negatively affecting her clients' returns. "When I brought it up to the company, their tone was immediately aggressive, 'No, we would have never agreed to that rate for you.' Luckily, I had it in writing. These situations came up time and again. I knew at the time, and I am positive today, that if I had been older or if I had been a guy, the exchange would have been different. When these conflicts arise in business, labels are often thrown at women, like 'Gosh, she's a bitch to work with.' Those tactics have the effect of making you self-conscious of your behavior. This comes despite the fact that you are only protecting your client's capital, and this is always correct behavior. It creates a distraction, *Am I being difficult?* Lauren learned to tune out these noisy distractions and not apologize for serving the interests of her investors.

When I asked her about intimidation in the industry, she claimed to actually find women more intimidating than men: "I tend to avoid the women's groups because, honestly, my experience has been that these groups can harbor really cutthroat people ... I try not to judge though, because I understand the experiences of women who have been in our industry for a while."

Mentoring and Teaching Financial Literacy

Lauren makes a point of educating her investors on value investing and the strategy. Once women work hard to earn a senior position, many will have to balance those responsibilities with the demands of their family life. Only after that can they focus on their desire to encourage younger women following a similar path. She recognizes the ways in which investing changed her life because she started at a young age, and she has a passion to share this gift with all young people who will listen. She often tells young people that they are the most powerful investors in the world because the "magic" of compounding is tremendously enhanced over a long period of time.

Philosophy

Lauren values financial literacy. From 2010 to 2012, she taught a behavioral finance course at the University of Tennessee in Chattanooga. Her firm remains conscious of, and attempts to correct, the often-poor messaging from the investment industry. She believes that investing is more understandable than people recognize, and it needs to become more publicly accessible. Lauren also believes the industry could do a better job of educating young people about the pros (compound interest) and cons (credit card debt) of finance: "Compounding is magical, but the magic ingredient is time. Starting young is important and avoiding debt is critical. Young people possess the most precious resource for investing: time."

Margaret Rust

Lighthouses in Margaret's Words

"My dad inspired me from an early age to participate in the stock market. He taught me technical analysis, and I even charted stocks for him because back then, we didn't have computers! It was my dad who started studying financial planning as he was transitioning to a semi-retired life in his mid-50s. I joined him at UC Berkeley, and that's when Rubey & Rust was born. We started our business together in 1992, and he brought not only wisdom but all his friends (to be our clients) who knew that he "knew" what he was doing. I learned everything I know about technical analysis from him. Around 1998 we began studying for the CFA designation together and that really gave us entry to the investing world. Dad was my study buddy, and we had such fun working on our CFAs together.

My mom was a great example of a strong woman who fought for equal rights and equality in the academic world, and in the workplace, and, frankly, in every aspect of her life. She is a Ruth Bader Ginsburg in her own right. She set the example for education (she has degrees from Stanford, Harvard, and UC Berkeley) and never, ever settled for second best. She (and I) come from a long line of strong, independent women who left great marks on the world by being smart, classy, and stubborn as hell. I think I follow that mold pretty well.

My gram (my mom's mom) was one completely amazing woman as well, fighting each and every day to do what was right and what was kind. Born in 1905, she barely survived and then went on to live ninety-five years. She saw women get the vote and she graduated from the University of Wisconsin with a degree in economics! She lived many lives in her ninety-five years and was a great influence on me. "Always be a blessing in other people's lives": that was her mantra, and I try hard every day to follow her example. Neither of these women ever kept quiet if something needed to be said.

And I couldn't have done any of it without my wholly supportive husband, Harrold. He has always given me complete freedom to follow my dreams and pursue goals that weren't always logical when having and raising three children. He was always there helping and supporting. Now, almost thirty years later, those efforts have paid off, but there were lots of early years where it was all study or work and not much money. He's a gem through and through!

There are angels that watch over me (believe me they do!) and then there's Harrold: he's my angel in this life."

Early Years

Margaret Rust has always been fascinated with money. Childhood monetary gifts were saved or given to her parents for investment. She kept a journal of all the money she made from doing her various chores. Back in the 1970s, it was $0.25 for taking out the mail and $1.00 for practicing the piano or doing the dinner dishes. In 1976, when she was eleven, she begged her mom to help her open a checking account. Her friends thought she was crazy, but Margaret thought it was the coolest thing ever to be able to write a check. Her father worked in sales and marketing at IBM. He was always interested in the stock market and did lots of technical analysis in his free time. Margaret often went with him to his office in San Francisco to help him plot stock charts and make copies on a giant Xerox machine.

In high school, the glamour of the fashion industry attracted Margaret to take a summer job at Nordstrom. When she started college at UC Davis in 1983, she followed her infatuation with fashion, and majored in textiles and clothing. However, she never lost sight of finance. Her major was flexible and allowed for classes in accounting, finance, and investing. "I knew I had found my passion," she remembers. Women were not encouraged to seek jobs in finance, and she didn't have the confidence or support network to try a job in finance, so she "took the easy job" and returned to Nordstrom after graduation.

While Nordstrom was fun, it wasn't finance. Working as a department manager offered some challenges, but also frustrations. Margaret tried to encourage her colleagues to invest in their 401(k)s and employee stock purchase plans (ESPPs) and be conscious of their spending habits, ideas that most people did not learn about in school. First jobs are always enlightening, and the world is not always a friendly place, but taking care of the people who worked for her and gave her their loyalty and trust became a paramount priority for Margaret. After learning many lessons, including the fact that greed and ego often get in the way of quality management and leadership, Margaret left Nordstrom with a keen understanding that she wanted to work for herself. Observing how empowering good leadership can be motivated her to build a career in a place where she could really make a difference. Teaching and promoting financial literacy evolved into the approach she would take to run her advisory firm and take care of her clients.

As for most people, Margaret's early working years showcase a lot of personal growth, learning about limitations, and realizing dreams.

At Nordstrom, Margaret learned how important it was for managers to inspire loyalty in their employees, empower them, help them follow their dreams, and protect them. Some of her employees may have been working in retail because they did not have any other choices. As their manager, Margaret knew she had a chance to help them make a better life. One of her founding philosophies is "Save your money because money gives you choices and choices give you freedom." She remembers when, at twenty-four years old, she was told by a store manager to make some goals for herself and that "80 percent of reaching a goal is writing it down." So she wrote down, "I want to have $1 million by the time I am thirty-five years old." It seemed a lofty goal because at that time, she could not even qualify for a mortgage despite being gainfully employed and having the down-payment money. As a single woman, her father had to cosign her first mortgage.

Path to Success

During those same early years, Margaret's dad was preparing to retire from IBM, which offered retirees a program that paid them to get a degree in whatever discipline they wanted. As an investment guru, Margaret's dad chose financial planning. The two of them decided to go back to school together. As they both had day jobs, they attended UC Berkeley's graduate certificate program at night and graduated in 1992 with the Personal Financial Planning (PFP) certification. They couldn't wait to get started!

Rubey & Rust

At this point, Margaret left Nordstrom and with her father, Charles Rubey, founded Rubey & Rust Capital Management. To help launch their new venture, they found a small private broker dealer, Protected Investors of America. They joined the brokerage firm and rented office space. In order to acquire some initial clients, they sent out a letter to everyone they knew (email didn't exist in 1992), and because of the credibility her father brought to the table, they received responses immediately. "We never looked back," she remembers. "We were busy right away." Joining Protected Investors of America helped them tremendously, but it came with struggles. The financial industry was much more of a man's world then than it is now. The president at the time told her that she needed to "take her pretty face and sell mutual funds." She struggled with sexism in the beginning but held firm. At almost six feet tall, most men knew she was not to be messed with! Nevertheless, her lack of confidence nagged at her. Her new goal was a financial education beyond reproach: a chartered financial analyst (CFA) certification.

The Importance of a CFA

For the first few years, her dad was *the guy* at the firm and Margaret took care of the many administrative details required to run a practice. At twenty-seven years old, she decided she wanted something more. She wanted her dad's friends and their clients to respect her and her financial advice despite her young age. They were equal partners and, she felt, deserved equal attention in their roles. By this point, Margaret was married and was fortunate to not need to work. Her dad was officially retired, which meant they both had the freedom to work for the pure joy of the business and to study! And so began the goal of attaining the CFA designation, which is a rigorous process. It took her five years, all while bringing up her children. The tests are offered only once each year, and back then, levels two and three necessitated six-hour essay exams. But knowledge is power, and the CFA curriculum is extensive. Not only was her education improving but with a CFA after her name, Margaret noticed that doors were opening. She felt respected, and she gained the confidence she so desperately sought. Her biggest problem as a woman was that men questioned her credibility, but once they knew she was a CFA, her opinion mattered—and that felt great.

Growing the Business

A lot happened between Margaret's writing down her goal and her thirty-fifth birthday. She started a business, married, had three children, attained the CFA designation, and by the time she was thirty-five, her net worth was north of her $1 million goal. She had achieved that lofty, seemingly impossible dream. She worked tirelessly saving, investing, and taking charge of the family's finances. Years later, Margaret's daughter set a similar goal, and by the age of twenty-five, she, too, had saved enough to "walk away." Margaret always counsels, "Money gives you choices and choices give you freedom. If you run into a jerk, you need to have the money and the confidence to say, 'Wow!' and walk away."

Over time, life brought challenges as Margaret's mom got sick and her dad had to spend less time working in the business. Margaret moved the office to her house which, as it turned out, made the firm even more profitable. She jokes that "the parking is free, and the coffee is a *lot* better." After her mother recovered, her father began to work more regularly again, and even in 2019, her dad, now eighty-five, still does security analysis and flies down to California once a quarter to meet with clients.

Rubey & Rust's clients consist of anyone who needs good and honest advice. They range from the very wealthy, who don't need as much financial planning as they need investment management, to younger people who need their hands held. As of 2019, they are working to build a client base of millennials because "they are our future." Margaret's motto is "If you don't love dealing with your money, then hire her [Margaret], and she will love your money for you." Her husband has always been a tremendous support, taking care of the kids during those long study periods and giving her the freedom to work long hours at a low-paying job until Rubey & Rust Capital Management was truly established. When Rubey & Rust Capital Management became a strong and sustaining business, Margaret's husband had the financial freedom to start a company of his own. Now, they are grateful to both be working hard to make our world a better place.

Philosophy

Margaret's early work experience taught her the importance of setting personal and professional goals, and that the simple act of writing those goals down gives them power. Now, as she runs her firm, goal setting is an annual ritual. "What shall we accomplish this year?" is asked every January. Interestingly, those goals always materialize. Her guiding philosophies revolve around service, kindness, and empowerment. While she remains a woman in a man's industry, she takes pride in her accomplishments. Allowing herself to feel empowered is often as much a challenge as counseling others to be brave. Whether it be conferences or professional lectures, she knows she has earned the right to be there and to be heard. "I've always found other women to be very supportive and friendly and I strive to share my hard-built confidence with those who will follow."

Fran Skinner

Lighthouses in Fran's Words

"The first one without question that I would point to would be my husband. He is also in investments. He was doing his CFA exam when I switched over to finance. I knew pretty quickly that I was over my head because I did not have a lot of finance as an undergrad. I was taking his CFA 1 books and I was studying them in the evening, self-teaching myself finance, essentially. It worked. It worked like a dream. He was encouraging me to take the CFA exam, and he said, "You are doing the work. Just take the darn exam." I wouldn't do it for a couple of reasons. The first is I was pregnant with our second child and our first was only one and a half years old, and I felt like I did not have time to be taking tests and the pressure of that and working a full-time job.

Second, quite frankly in the back of my head I saw myself as an accountant in a room of qualified finance people who was pulling a fast one. If I took the test and I failed, they would figure it out. So, I wouldn't take the test. When I was on maternity leave, a big package arrived in the mail. It was from the CFA Institute welcoming me into the CFA program. My husband signed me up. He did his tough love talk with me about how I am holding myself back. He was still doing the program himself, so now it would be both of us studying, working full-time, and raising two boys. Thanks to him as that lighthouse, he basically forced me to see my negative self-talk. Thanks to him and his support, I passed all the exams on the first try, and that was a huge door opener for me in terms of going back and overcoming that small school bias by being one of only 18 percent of CFAs who are women [as of 2016]. He's a keeper."

Early Years

In high school, Fran Skinner had an ever-growing passion for theatre. She spent her free time acting in school plays and skits. For most of her time in high school, she believed she would become a professional actress. However, Fran is the first generation in her family to go to college, so she decided that she needed to study something other than theatre in order to have a stable profession. In the neighborhood of Chicago where she grew up, college was a special opportunity. Many of her peers stayed at home, worked in the family grocery store or other places, and went to college on a part- or full-time basis.

Fran started out studying elementary education at Saint Xavier University in 1982. After six grueling months as an elementary education major, Fran started to take business classes and ended up changing her major to business administration. As graduation approached, Fran decided she wanted to graduate with more than a degree to improve her chances of getting a job, so she took the CPA exam to become an accountant. She earned her BA in 1986 from a small school in Chicago. However, where she received her education became a challenge to her career. She said, "I got an amazing education at my college, but it was a huge uphill battle coming from an unknown school until I got my MBA. It was hard to command respect when you came from a small school that no one heard of ... I had no conception how much that would haunt me early in my career."

Fran's degree led her to asset-based auditing at Mellon Bank in the Financial Services division. Fran did due diligence on customers' finances. She stayed with auditing for ten months before she realized how much she did not enjoy it. She joined the Allstate Insurance Company's investment accounting team and thrived in her new position. But when she had the opportunity to leave investment accounting for investment administration, Fran jumped at the chance. Her new job allowed her to work across the firm in a management position. Six years later, Fran became a director who acted as a consultant to the CIO in investment resource management. She worked at Allstate for a total of sixteen and a half years, and while she was working there, Fran earned her MBA in Finance and Marketing at the University of Illinois in Chicago in 2002.

Her decision to leave Allstate did not please her father. She said, "I told my dad, who was an immigrant and grew up during the Depression, that I was leaving Allstate. He thought I was wildly successful when I got that job, and that I was set for life. When I told him I was leaving, he grabbed his head, and he told me to leave the room. I was a professional young adult with two children, but he couldn't talk to me because he was so upset that I was leaving the stability of my job. I just knew there was a lot more to my world than playing it safe. I felt the pull to go and see what else was out there."

Path to Success

Every position Fran had held made her more passionate about working with individuals to improve a company. "We tend to put great investors into people-management roles without realizing that might not be the best idea." Fran left Allstate to start her own consulting firm in 2003 called Focus Consulting Group. She worked as an independent consultant to senior leaders of investment firms under the Focus

Consulting Group umbrella. During her time there, Fran, along with three of her peers, published a book called *High Performing Investment Teams: How to Achieve Best Practices of Top Firms.* She developed leadership coaching and training to help each firm attain their objectives.

Fran used what she learned throughout her career to help firms find the best fit for their job openings either from outside or from internal promotions. "The big key is not trying to fit square pegs in a round hole. One of the mottos I use at my firm is from our job fit matrix: we are looking for the intersection of eligibility and suitability. Eligibility is: Can I do the job? Do I have the degrees, the certification? etc. Suitability is: Do I want to do the job? I go back to my history when I think about this. That's where my passion for this work comes from. I could have been an elementary school teacher, but I would've been absolutely miserable." Throughout her career, she has known many great investors who were put into management roles that did not fit them, often because they did not want a management role or because they were not interested in improving their poor management skills.

Most of the time, Fran told me in our interview, the people who were reporting to these misfit managers were pretty miserable as well. At Allstate, in her resource management role, she worked with managers to find the best-fitting people for the roles. She is unique because she understands both sides: investment and management. As she explains, "It was a unique experience because a lot of investment people do not value soft skills. They are not looking for cookie cutter consultants to come in and tell them what works. I had a unique edge because I had sat in their chairs, whether it was operations, accounting, or asset allocation. I had the same credentials that they did with the CFA and the CPA and the MBA. They would give me that moment to get started, and that was all I needed because then, I went back to my high school years of acting training to grab and keep their attention throughout my training, coaching, or presentations to audiences."

Diamond Hill

Fran left Focus Consulting Group in 2009 to cofound her own firm, AUM Partners, and in 2010, she became an independent member of the Corporate Governance board of Diamond Hill Investment Group, a member of the Audit Committee, and chair of the Compensation Committee. Diamond Hill is a publicly traded investment firm. Her role on the board let her oversee the succession of Diamond Hill's first CEO and provide the CEO with an annual performance review. She was on the board until the new CEO approached her in 2018 to offer her the position of chief administrative officer for investments. Upon her appointment, Chris Bingman, then CEO, observed, "Fran has a long-standing relationship with Diamond Hill as a consultant and corporate board member; she shares our values and long-term philosophy. She will be instrumental to our firm's continued growth, with her role primarily focused on optimizing our investment team structure and succession planning, as well as coaching and development." Fran accepted this opportunity to be a member of Diamond Hill's leadership team. She consulted with the leadership and investment team to create a sustainable and positive impact on Diamond Hill.

Continuing to Develop Leaders at AUM Partners

In September 2019, Fran decided to return to AUM Partners to share her abilities in consulting and financial-services leadership training: "I discovered that my true passion is helping lots of people be happy and successful in their careers."

Philosophy

Fran's approach continues to help companies and individuals become more successful by organizing and placing the right people in the right places. This combination builds on Fran's deep industry experience and identifies cultural, leadership, and management attributes and structures to maximize effectiveness. By ensuring that her clients have the best possible fit with advisors, Fran helps develop leaders and leading organizations.

Sonya Dreizler

Lighthouses in Sonya's Words

"I had a couple mentors at the beginning of my career, and as my career progressed, I got to have more and more. Now many of my peers are also mentors, and I feel like I am surrounded. I love my network of kick-ass women in finance. I can ask them for guidance, favors, or introductions as needed, and they often give me perspective even when I don't ask, which I really appreciate.

I had a couple of really good bosses, one woman and one man. That would be it in the beginning of my career. My dad has given me guidance through the years because he has been in the business. When I was younger, I wanted to be independent from my dad and not be "Bob's daughter." I wanted to be my own person. Now I just want to hang out with my dad.

Another lighthouse: When I was new to the consulting business, a journalist interviewed me. After the interview published, we got to know each other and became good business friends. She coached me on social media at a time I needed it and that has paid off well for me. We are still close.

I have a dear friend who is a regulatory and compliance expert who can quickly point me in the right direction when I have a question and is also a good friend for talking about big-picture business issues. There are just so many, so many amazing women that I count on as well as a handful of men."

Early Years

Throughout Sonya's entire life, she was surrounded by finance. Her father, Bob Dreizler, was a pioneer in socially responsible investing (SRI), so Sonya was constantly reminded of the importance of aligning values with spending and investing habits. Her father introduced Sonya to impact investing where she found her passion, and her mother was her "role model for succeeding as a woman in an overwhelmingly male business, and for running a client-centered business with kindness and integrity."

Sonya's mother is an entrepreneur. She opened her own physical therapy business after her boss was unwilling to pay her as much as her male coworkers. Sonya observed the whole process from creating a business plan to seeing the first clinic. She watched her mom's business triple in size. She watched as her mom was continually treated as inferior to the men in her field. She began to ask questions about the day-to-day operations of the business, which quickly led to her mother consulting her on "negotiating challenging employee issues, systems organization, marketing, and positioning the business for a manageable amount of growth."

Though she was surrounded by the world of finance, Sonya was not interested in starting to invest during her childhood. She attended the University of California, Los Angeles, and earned her degree in English, Spanish, and Latin American Studies. She still had little interest in finance.

After she graduated in 2002, Sonya landed a job as an escrow assistant at LandAmerica Commonwealth, which she quickly realized she was not passionate about and left the position after a year. As she searched for another opportunity, she found an opening for an executive assistant and event planner for Protected Investors of America. She applied but made it clear in her interview that she was not interested in financial services. Even with that disclaimer, she was offered the job on the spot, and she made a one-year commitment.

One of the many responsibilities of her position was to create portfolio reports, and as she did not know a lot about investing at the time, she had to do quite a bit of searching on Investopedia. The position allowed her to learn the ways the company operated. The CEO who hired her threw her into the deep end, and she did well. As she explained, "I learn by doing and I often had to learn the hard way. I did well, and she gave me more responsibilities and encouraged me to restructure and create efficient processes and procedures in each department."

Path to Success

After three years as an executive assistant, Sonya was promoted to the position of vice president of Advisor Services, under the same CEO. Only two years later, she was promoted to the position of chief operations officer (COO). She enjoyed the hands-on aspect of COO work. She liked consulting with each department within the company and improving their efficiency. Five years later, she applied for the chief financial officer (CFO) position and was promoted to that role.

CEO of Protected Investors of America

Sonya's progression continued all the way to the top when, four years later, the CEO left the company, and she decided to apply for the open position. She was hired as CEO of Protected Investors of America eleven years after being hired as the executive assistant. "I wouldn't have gotten as far as I did in this business without the first woman who hired me, pushed me beyond my comfort zone, and had more faith in my ability to learn than I had in myself at the time."

Throughout her time as the CEO, Sonya enjoyed running the business, but she did not enjoy the investing part of it. She was working so hard that she wasn't taking care of herself, became stressed, and did not have a lot of time to spend with her kids. She didn't realize it until she left the company to become a consultant.

Finding Her Voice in Consulting

Sonya wanted to use her voice and experience to help underrepresented people in the finance industry. As she explained: "Being familiar with how clients interact with investments and knowing financial services from the ground up lets me come in and be helpful in a pragmatic way." At Protected Investors, she learned the importance of personal connections, personal integrity, and hard work, all of which paid off over time. Because of her network, she is able to connect her clients with the resources they need. Well-established in her career, she enjoys more financial independence and the greater trust people place in her because of her solid experience. This, she feels, gives her opportunities she didn't have early in her professional life.

Philosophy

Sonya works to make a rapidly evolving field understandable. She enjoys consulting because it enables her to express what she is passionate about, such as socially responsible (SRI) investing, and environmental, social, and governance (ESG) investing, a modern term for impact investing, which Sonya learned from her father. (See Appendix A for descriptions of these types of investing).

Vicki Saunders

<u>Lighthouses in Vicki's Words</u>

"I have many. I am struck by wisdom and truth telling, so when I hear someone say something that wakes me up, I collect it and add it to my list. I'm a synthesizer. I feel like I've been following the breadcrumbs one by one and some day it will all be clear. There is no one thing. It's a series of books, articles, conversations, relationships, tuning into subtle energies, paying attention to what moves me and what doesn't. It's a very personal path. There is no right answer for everyone. The path is to find your truth. I could list a whole bunch of things, and what you really need to know is to hone your own intuition and find your own path. Keep moving, every day."

Early Years

Vicki grew up on a pick-your-own farm in Canada. Throughout her childhood, she witnessed how a small business operates day to day, but at that time, the business narrative was about big corporations rather than entrepreneurship. So, Vicki did not put two and two together until later in her life: small business entrepreneurs can make changes in the world.

Vicki's experience on the farm helped her develop a strong work ethic, resilience, and creativity that became important for her career. From an early age, she wanted to make a change in the world. This was why she studied comparative foreign policy at the University of Toronto.

After graduating in 1989, she was not quite sure what she wanted to do with her life and decided to expand her horizons. She traveled to Prague right after the Berlin Wall came down. During the four years she was there, she noticed a new way of thinking. People were stepping back from their lives, asking, "Now that I'm free, what am I going to do?" This way of thinking dramatically shifted the way Vicki thought about her future. She has always struggled with limiting herself. I asked her about the rose, a joy, and thorn, a woe, in her life. She gave the same answer for both questions: "I am the only one limiting me. There is no one else." What she witnessed in Prague will forever stay with her and cause her to push her limits.

Path to Success

Vicki took her innovative spirit and cofounded Kids NRG in 1997. Kids NRG was a youth entrepreneurship initiative that hired youth to market and design products and services for their age group. In 1999, Vicki expanded her initial company to include an incubator, The NRG Group. Vicki grew her team from eight to sixty-five people in less than two years. The NRG Group was a consulting group for young entrepreneurs who sought help to create next-generation Internet companies. Vicki cofounded Impactanation in 2001. This initiative offered youthful solutions for global issues. From 2001 to 2008, Impactanation had many successes including developing a global water initiative for Schlumberger, an oilfield services company, and WaterEngage, a water education initiative with the McLaughlin Rotman Centre for Global Health, and the organization engaged youth in global nonprofits and for-profits to find solutions to world problems. In 2007, she founded Zazengo, a platform for employees of various companies including Walmart, Johnson & Johnson, and Coca-Cola and consumers to take steps toward sustainability.

In 2010, she left Zazengo and became a senior advisor at MaRS Discovery District, Canada's largest accelerator of start-ups in clean tech, life science, information and communications technology (ICT) and social innovation. This gave her the opportunity to work on the other side of start-ups advising high-potential start-ups that were strong socially and financially. She worked as a senior advisor for a little under two years and then joined the Council of Canadian Academies as an expert on the Socio-Economic Impacts of Innovation Investments panel until 2013.

Supporting Women Entrepreneurs at SheEO

In 2015, Vicki founded SheEO, a global initiative to change the ways we support female entrepreneurs and create connections between advisors and innovators: "Our SheEO Community is based on being radically generous with ourselves and others. If we show up with that practice every day, I believe we will transform ourselves and the world." The SheEO community is comprised of around 4,000 women, called activators, who contribute $1,100 annually. The money is pooled and loaned at a low interest rate to five ventures voted on by the activators. The loans are paid back over five years, and those funds are then loaned out to other ventures, creating an ongoing fund.

SheEO's mission is to radically redesign the ecosystem that supports, finances, and celebrates female innovators. The proof is in the portfolio of companies that SheEO helped launch and grow. It is a testament to the creative power of the thousands of female entrepreneurs who built the businesses. The SheEO family of companies runs the gamut from health care to technology to consumer products to social ventures, and more.

Through 2019, the impact of SheEO has been substantial for many women and woman-run businesses. During our interview, Vicki told me that the 4,000 activators have loaned over $4 million to fifty-three business ventures in five countries. Companies that are not voted to be financially supported are still supported by the SheEO community. Vicki creates networks between the entrepreneurs and other professionals, hoping to provide them with the support they need to grow. The ripple effects get wider from there, each business venture creates around three jobs, on average, per year. Through her work, Vicki has found a way to make real change in the world.

Yet she is not satisfied. Her goals for SheEO are to continue growing it to one million activators supporting over $1 billion in loans to 10,000 business ventures with tens of thousands of jobs created.

Throughout her experiences as an innovator, Vicki has observed that the environment dictates how individuals and companies thrive. The mindset of "anything is possible" that surrounded her in Prague was empowering, but when she returned to Canada, a few years later, to develop her start-up, a lot of people told her that she thought "too big," and they advised her to "start small," with a pilot. However, later, on a trip to Silicon Valley, she was encouraged to develop her start-up at twice the speed with twice as much money.

Philosophy

Vicki learned that the environment is not the only deciding factor for a start-up. Leadership is crucial in starting a sustainable company: "A good leader notices what lights people up, creates the space for those people to stay in that zone as their 'role' and gets out of the way so magic can happen. We all need to be cared for to reach our potential. We are social. We will go much further together when we are connected than when we are isolated and feeling alone." Creating an ecosystem where innovation can thrive requires connections between what she calls learn-it-alls, the opposite of know-it-alls. Learn-it-alls have a growth mindset that is crucial to tackling new problems.

Each experience Vicki Saunders has had as an innovator has been different, and all her experiences have come with individual hardships and joyous moments. Deep down, Vicki knows this is the only path for her, and she has tried every day to make a change: "I was born unemployable by anyone else. I need space to experiment, to try new things, to follow the energy, to change my mind four times a day, to iterate and make a mess, and then reflect on what feels right and what doesn't. The journey to this point has been a very winding path full of learning and failure and struggle and a few little successes along the way but/and I'm nowhere near where I want to be as a person, a leader, a partner. I have so much work to do. And if today was my last day on the planet, I'd be okay with that too. I'm not done, but I've given everything I've got every day."

Leaders

Heather Brilliant

Lighthouses in Heather's Words

"For the first five to eight years of my career, I benefited from the mentorship of Bill Andersen, former portfolio manager at Driehaus [Capital Management], where I worked. He is now founding principal of Ranger International, and we stay in touch to this day. Bill was so helpful thinking through my different career moves. I trust and value his opinions.

Joe Mansueto, founder and chairman of Morningstar, where I worked for almost fourteen years, was also a lighthouse. He is such an inspiring leader because he had a vision for how he wanted to transform investing and was extremely successful at implementing his vision. He thought about the competitive advantage of the company he created and made decisions based on the long term—more so than many entrepreneurs. He did not do everything perfectly. He would be the first to admit that, which is another great quality of his. He has always been an accessible leader."

Early Years

Heather Brilliant was introduced to investing at a young age and began her career at Bank of America as a corporate finance analyst covering the auto industry. In 2003, Heather joined Morningstar, a leading provider of independent investment research, as a research analyst. She covered a wide variety of sectors, eventually rising to head of equity research.

Heather's career progressed to leadership roles in the investment industry as CEO of Morningstar Australasia, CEO Americas of First State Investments, and now CEO of Diamond Hill Capital Management. Diamond Hill is a long-term-focused investment management firm that serves individual investors, advisors, and institutions. Upon Heather's appointment at Diamond Hill, James F. Laird, chair of the board of directors, observed, "Heather brings an in-depth understanding of the investment management industry and significant leadership experience to Diamond Hill, and we believe she is a strong cultural fit. Our industry is undergoing a period of significant change, and we are confident in Heather's ability to lead us into the future."

Heather's focus on serving the long-term interests of individual investors goes back a long way. In particular, Heather's female family role models had a lot to do with her path in investing and leadership. Her mother, Peg, paved the way to her leadership aspirations.

"I was fortunate to have a mother who had an MBA," Heather explained, "which was unusual at the time. Her achievements empowered me to think I could do anything and take on any kind of career opportunity."

Heather's mother was unique in many ways. She was an entrepreneur who started several businesses.

"Her most successful business was a video production company where she would film weddings or parties and edit the videos. This might sound basic in this day and age where everybody can take a video with their smart phone, but it was unusual back then," she said.

Her grandmother, Helen, was a role model as an investor. Heather's grandfather passed away at a young age. Her grandmother had to take over the family finances and manage her family of seven children. Left with a nest egg, she began investing and quickly learned what it meant to be a savvy investor at a time when women rarely touched their own finances. She invested mainly in large capitalization equities and real estate in a style similar to Warren Buffett and she always had a small number of long-term investments, around twenty holdings, mostly in blue-chip stocks. Her investing success was due to her temperament and long-term focus, and her sage investing abilities introduced Heather to the world of investing. Not all investors have the qualities to become as successful at investing as Heather's grandmother was, and Heather realized early in her career that the investment industry could do more to help people reach their financial goals.

In addition to teaching Heather how to invest, Heather's grandmother taught her the importance of asserting herself. One of her favorite stories is about her grandmother's stockbroker: "I'll never forget when she told me that she had a broker who executed her trades. She trusted this guy, and she worked with him for years. One day, he made a trade without clearing it with her, and she fired him immediately. She was so angry. She said, 'He did not think I could make the decision, and it's my money. He didn't have the authority to make that decision on my behalf.'" Heather's grandmother was decisive and confident and recognized that individual investors could benefit from taking an active role in managing their portfolios.

Path to Success

Heather grew up in the Chicago area and stayed there through college and business school. After spending a year in Spain, her interest in international markets began to grow. Her first few jobs as an analyst were focused on covering several sectors in the pharmaceutical and retail industries in international markets. She did not have a science background and had never enjoyed science in school, but she did enjoy the challenge of analyzing the health-care sector.

"I had to get up to speed on all of the different parts of pharmaceutical and biotech treatments, not just the financial aspects, but how to analyze and think about different clinical trial results and how [a company could] be successful in the health-care space," she said. The plethora of sectors Heather covered helped her as she rose to a leadership role at Morningstar in 2005. It is also a great example of the benefits of learning about a new industry, even when it stems from a topic that might not have been a passion during school.

Before becoming Morningstar's CEO of Australasia, Heather was the global head of equity and credit research. She and her team screened for wide-moat companies (those with strong competitive advantages) by looking first for quantitative evidence of possible moats such as high profit margins and return on equity. The analysts then evaluated the qualitative aspects of a company's competitive advantage.

"The investment research process goes beyond finding solid companies," Heather said. "They must also be a good value."

International Investing

Heather became more and more interested in international investing during her time at Morningstar. The original Morningstar Wide Moat Focus index looked for high-quality companies but, for the most part, was restricted to US markets. Heather helped refine Morningstar's moat strategy globally by expanding its international presence in equity research. This allowed the principles of buying quality companies at fair prices to be applied to companies in Europe and Asia.

The Issue of Gender Diversity

Heather has taken on leadership roles that have often meant she was the only woman in a meeting. In the beginning of her career, she didn't spend much time thinking about the lack of gender diversity in the industry. "I didn't know any better," she said. For the most part, her experiences had been good with the exception of an early job interview.

"I was pregnant with my first child and I was interviewing for a job in New York. I was based in Chicago at the time. The interview went well, and the portfolio manager wanted me to fly to New York for an in-person interview. I said, 'That is wonderful, and I would love to. I want you to know before I come out that I am five months pregnant. That won't affect my ability to perform this role in any way, but I thought you should be aware.' He was suddenly busy the following week, and there was no way he could possibly make time. He would be in touch with me as soon as he could, which turned into never."

When she moved to Australia and realized that the industry, overall, had a long way to go in promoting gender diversity, she decided to get more involved. Heather encourages women to take on leadership roles especially in professions and industries where gender diversity is lacking. She makes herself accessible to people inside and outside her firm. Her advice for young women in the industry: "Raise your hand. It's important to figure out what you want to do and to make that known. As much as I hate to generalize, I have seen women less willing to put their hands up and express their interest in taking on a new role or taking their career in a new direction."

Her Development as a Leader

As her career progressed from analyst to research head to CEO, Heather grew as a leader. She has a keen focus on company culture. "It is critically important to set the course for your company and where you want to go, and to communicate that effectively to your team and help them feel connected and part of that mission," she says.

Heather tries to live by Australian General David Morrison's mantra: "The standard you walk past is the standard you accept." Leaders need to set the bar for the behaviors that define their team culture and enforce behavior expectations consistently.

As CEO, Heather thinks as an owner/investor does, taking a long-term view. Much of a CEO's job is focused on empowering others, allocating capital, and managing risk appropriately. "Over time, as I have become more comfortable with different aspects of risk, I try to take calculated risks where there is an asymmetric payoff opportunity. Taking risks is a critical part of being a leader."

Even as her career progressed, Heather continued to learn through analyzing companies, making investment decisions, and constructing portfolios. "As an investor, it's critical to be as open minded as possible while having conviction. That balance is what separates an average analyst from a great one." The same qualities that make successful investors, such as careful analysis and long-term thinking, also make successful CEOs.

Philosophy

In her interview on *After Hours*, an Australian video series featuring women in the financial services industry, Heather said, "There is a lack of trust in the financial services industry that has caused people to be more interested in investing on their own than in trusting a system that they feel has let them down. We have to make sure we align the interests of the intermediaries with the end investor. We need to focus on offering products that are in the best interest of investors in a timeframe when they will be helpful to investors. We know from studies done at Morningstar that many investors will invest at the peak of market cycles, for example, and that fund companies tend to launch new products at the peak which encourages that investor to come into the market at exactly the wrong time. We need to treat the investor fairly and not take fees just because we can."

Heather also serves on the board of the CFA Institute, a premiere organization for investment professionals that administers the rigorous Chartered Financial Analyst program. She has traveled the globe to promote the CFA Institute's purpose, which is to "create an environment where investors' interests come first, markets function at their best, and economies grow."

Heather is passionate about helping the investment industry continue to improve diversity efforts and ensuring that individual investors are treated fairly. She considers herself a lifelong learner and just as she has learned from other leaders and mentors, she aspires to be a lighthouse to those around her.

Denise Strack

Lighthouses in Denise's Words

"In looking back, several women have acted as a lighthouse for me over the years. Starting with a high school math teacher, to a college professor, my first boss, and several other amazing women that have mentored and supported me throughout my career. They all brought their authentic selves to work every day, embracing career, family, and community. I am forever grateful for their leadership and support, and I hope I can do the same for others in the future."

Early Years

Finance was not a part of Denise Strack's family's daily discussion. Denise was born into a multigenerational family of farmers in Ohio. Her grandfather, who did not have a college education, traded commodities such as corn and soybeans, which meant that he traded to protect his crop from commodity price changes.

Denise's interests in high school, however, were not agricultural. Her passion was in math and science due to two teachers who pushed her passion: Ms. Chambers, her calculus teacher, and Mr. Merryweather, her biology teacher. Throughout high school, she was an avid gymnast. She was a member of the US National Gymnastics Team and was one of the top twenty gymnasts in the USA. Gymnastics taught Denise lifelong skills of endurance, concentration, long-term goal setting, and balancing life and work efficiently. She said, "I developed a way of focusing on what matters, what is important, not letting the other noise distract me, and using every minute to its fullest."

Stanford

Denise was accepted at Stanford with an athletic scholarship and an interest in getting a math major. That interest did not stick. She quickly decided that she did not want to be a math major in part because of how few women there were in the math program. Denise transferred to the engineering department to study for an industrial engineering major because a few of the professors were women, and she would have at least a few more female peers. Industrial engineering also felt more practical to her, and she could incorporate her passion for math with the finance part of the curriculum.

After graduating from Stanford University with a BS in Industrial Engineering in 1992, she decided to go to business school at age twenty-seven. That decision put her life on hold for quite a few years. As she observed, "It was an interesting point to put the pause button on the family aspect of my life. The part that I did not realize was that when you graduate from business school, you have a couple of years of a pretty intense career commitment that again postpones family and children."

Path to Success

Denise started working as an engagement manager at McKinsey & Company in the private equity and financial services practice for two years, right after graduating from business school, and then returned to work on Stanford's endowment as the director of private equity for two years.

Gordon and Betty Moore Foundation

During that time, the Gordon and Betty Moore Foundation was establishing itself. The foundation gives grants for environmental conservation, patient care, and science. The CIO for the Gordon & Betty Moore Foundation, at the time, was Alice Ruth. She reached out to Denise to join the foundation as the director of private equity and real assets in 2002. (Real-asset investments are tangible investments such as real estate, land, and precious metals.) Around that time, Denise was pregnant with her first child. She did not know what to expect as a reaction from Alice, but when Alice "jumped out of her chair, shouted congratulations, and gave her a big hug," it was transformational for Denise. "I decided to do the same for every woman who ever worked for me and was expecting," she said.

Six years later, Alice left the foundation for a different job opportunity, and Denise was not only appointed as CIO but quickly had to guide the foundation through the financial crisis in 2008, all while pregnant with her second daughter, who was born on September 18, the day after Lehman Brothers filed for bankruptcy. To establish herself as the CIO, she used what she had learned as a member of the US National Gymnastics Team along with her ability to block out noise and persist through challenges. Her success has not come without struggles such as starting a family while working to get her MBA.

Denise told me that when she was first promoted to the CIO position, the foundation was worth $4.5 billion. In 2016, and despite the challenges in 2008, the foundation was worth $6.9 billion, in part, due to the success of the foundation's venture capital and real estate investments. The foundation's employees have worked there for an average of nine years, which, as Denise says, "makes us unique in the industry because we can deploy with a long-term mind-set."[9] She enjoys working for the foundation because being a part of it and the "nonprofit mission makes the world a better place." During her time there, the foundation has given away $2.44 billion in grants.

Philosophy

Just as she learned to balance high school and gymnastics, Denise has learned to ignore the noise of others: "I have pursued my life as who I am. I have been in an environment where that has been fine, and I have not worried about every comment or where I sit at the table or every small gesture by others that may not be perfect. I just do what I do, and I do it well without being worried about the noise. In reality, I have been true to myself, without worrying too much about what other people think. If you walk in with a level of confidence, they pick up on that and don't second-guess you. If you come in expecting them to second-guess you, then they probably will. I have had people say inappropriate things or dismiss me, but in my mind that's noise. I can be effective if I maintain my confidence." Her biggest challenge throughout her career has been negotiating compensation to insure equal pay for equal work.

Lisa Shalett

Lighthouses in Lisa's Words

"I have been very lucky to have had a number of lighthouses over the course of my career and life. At different stages, each has had different lessons to teach me, and increasingly over time, the notion that a lighthouse needs to be someone more experienced or "senior" shifted to a definition that has largely included peers as well as "reverse mentor" types of lighthouses —younger people I have learned a lot from.

The two lighthouses I will name that correspond most to my career story you just described are two amazing, incredible people I got to know over the course of my career at Goldman Sachs. One was Mark Schwartz and the other, Suzanne Nora Johnson. I still feel very close to, and inspired by, each of them. When I got to know Mark, he was the vice chairman running Asia and based in Tokyo for Goldman Sachs, and I was, at the time, a VP based in New York, responsible for the North American institutional client base for the Japanese equities. When I got to know Suzanne, she had recently moved from investment banking to become the global cohead of investment research, and I had just become partner in the Equities Division and had returned from a stint in Tokyo to work for her as global head of equities merchandising.

Both got to know me by seeing me in action in my role. Both made it clear that they accepted me, were invested in me, and believed in me, unconditionally—and in doing so they gave me confidence, honest feedback, a safe space to come with questions and issues, an opportunity for dialogue and an exchange of ideas, and they always made time for me. It is worth noting that in both of these instances I was not in a junior role when they came into my life—yet I still benefited tremendously from knowing that people like them, whom I respected tremendously and who were highly regarded, respected me, and were in my corner. I know that they each had a big impact on my career and opportunities I was given. We should never underestimate the importance of lighthouses in instilling confidence; often we are our own worst enemies and undermine our own self-confidence and need others to help us regain confidence we should have. Their example has inspired me to be that kind of lighthouse for other people—to let them know they have to earn my respect, but once they do, I am *invested*, and I believe in them, and am there for them in any way I can be."

Early Years

Lisa Shalett had never considered a career in finance. In fact, a high school trip to Japan led her to major in East Asian studies and learn Japanese in college, and she followed that passion to her first job. She began her professional career in Tokyo at a Japanese television network, working as a production assistant on a hit game show. Wanting to learn more about finance, Lisa decided to go back to school and get her MBA. Eventually, she found Wall Street and worked as an associate in Japanese equities at Barclays in New York, and then at Goldman Sachs, where her career progressed from Japanese equities to partner and, eventually, head of brand marketing and digital strategy.

In college, her choice of a liberal arts major in East Asian studies was inspired by a high school experience as an exchange student in Japan. The Japanese family she lived with did not speak English, and she did not speak any Japanese. This cross-cultural immersion inspired her to learn Japanese so that one day she would be able to return to Japan and have conversations with that family. By the time she graduated from Harvard, summa cum laude, Japan was beginning its economic boom, and her sentimental decision to major in East Asian studies looked prescient. However, she wasn't really sure how to think about her career going forward with that expertise. She assumed only economics majors could go into finance.

Japanese Enterprises

Lisa was chosen for an internship created by the Fujisankei Communications Group, Japan's largest media company, which saw taking Ivy League interns as a way to help the company internationalize. From 1988 to 1991, Lisa lived in Tokyo and worked as a production assistant on a very popular Japanese television show, "Naruhodo! The World" which was an "edu-tainment" travelogue and game show that helped Japanese viewers in Japan learn about other cultures and customs around the world. She also was the business development associate on a home shopping show that "helped introduce and sell to the Japanese viewership new-to-Japan foreign products that were unique and had great stories about how they were made or used."

She moved back to New York in 1991 and continued working for Fujisankei in business development in their overseas headquarters to help expand their business opportunities in America and spot emerging trends for their subsidiaries in Japan. While in that role, Lisa recognized the opportunity to help educate the Japanese expatriate community who were adjusting to living in the New York-Connecticut-New Jersey area. She developed, wrote, produced, found a sponsor for, and appeared in a

Japanese television show on Fujisankei's local TV network that focused on healthy living topics.

MBA and New York

During this time, she took notice of her peers. Most of those she graduated with were in finance. "They were doing things where they seemed to be learning a trade, an approach, a methodology, a skill. It got to the point where sometimes I couldn't even understand the words they were using, and it made me really want to learn business ... They were learning skills that would help them be analytical, understand certain contexts, be professional, be able to understand a strategy ... They were being exposed to things that I didn't understand." Lisa realized she wanted to close this gap and decided to do something she never thought she would do: go back to school to get an MBA. By the time she got to Harvard Business School (HBS), the Japanese market had imploded and the expertise that had differentiated her and been a "competitive advantage"—understanding Japanese language, culture and business— was no longer in much demand.

However, a German media company, Bertelsmann, knew of Fujisankei and valued her experience there. They hired her through their MBA graduate program to become the assistant to the president of Bertelsmann Direct, which developed, managed, and distributed a number of Bertelsmann's music and video products. Given her background, she was asked to develop and launch the Japanese version of the company's very successful music distribution business model in Japan. However, she quickly discovered that the type of marketing, called negative option direct marketing, was not yet legal in Japan, and had to break the news that it couldn't be done. Instead, she was given a new strategic project, to negotiate a joint venture with Blockbuster to develop a video distribution club that would enable Bertelsmann to compete in the US market. While an interesting challenge, it was not at all related to Japan, and Lisa found that she really missed doing work that could leverage her background. This led her to start looking outside the company for a Japan-related job.

Path to Success

Lisa discovered Japanese equity sales through a newsletter mailed out by HBS to its alumni with career listings. In describing the skills required, the listing made it clear that it valued an understanding of Japanese language, culture, and business, rather than direct experience on Wall Street. She joined Barclays de Zoete Wedd in New York as a Japanese equities sales associate: "I couldn't believe I found a job where they would pay me to talk to smart people about Japan all day, value all my skills in Japanese culture and business, and teach me whatever I needed to know about the markets. That is how I stumbled my way onto Wall Street." Lisa quickly "fell in love with the dynamism of the trading floor, the challenge of finding the value amidst the noise, and the opportunity to help institutional investors identify and evaluate investment ideas in difficult foreign markets."

Japanese Equities Sales at Goldman Sachs

After working at Barclays for a year and a half, she moved to Goldman Sachs and continued in Japanese equity sales, proving herself to be very skilled at developing strong client relationships. The Japan Desk was small on the New York trading floor compared to the vast amount of space dedicated to US equities. Since Japan's market is active during the USA's nighttime, she spoke to clients in "dead" market hours: "The challenge was how to get clients in US hours to focus on Japan when the market wasn't open, how to create urgency and relevance." Lisa credits this experience with building her creativity and patience. "There was one very important client it took me a year to actually speak live to. Every day I would leave a voicemail for this client. The voicemail was limited to sixty seconds. You could re-record it if you screwed up and inevitably got cut off mid-sentence, and some mornings I would try multiple times to make my message fit (often prompting some laughter from my desk mates). But I was determined to find a way to succeed with this client; it became an obsessive personal goal. So, each day I would try to leave the perfect sixty-second voicemail, never knowing whether the client ever actually listened to this voicemail or if it went into deep space or if there was ever going to be a return on that investment. Let me tell you, sixty seconds is not a long period of time for a voicemail! I would do it over and over; I often felt like an idiot, but I still did it. A year later—maybe the client timed it to see if I lasted a year—but in literally a year to the day, that client picked up the phone. I didn't even know what to do. I didn't believe it. I was leaving my voicemail, and the person said, 'That sounds very interesting, Lisa.' I froze and could barely speak! Fortunately, I recovered, and from that day on I had a relationship with this client. Going through that, I definitely had a lot of lows figuring out if I had chosen the right profession, wondering if this was a waste of my time—and lo and behold, the persistence and dedication paid off."

Lisa worked her way up in Japanese equities from associate to VP and head of the Japanese Equities Sales Desk in North America, based in New York, to managing director and global head of the

Japanese Equities Sales and Trading Division, a role requiring relocation to Tokyo from 2000 to 2002. She took her husband and two young sons overseas as well. While managing a team around the world, she led some of the biggest global IPOs, managed important client relationships, grew revenues and Goldman Sachs's broker rankings, and worked closely with the Global Investment Research team to identify franchise-defining investment ideas for clients. In 2002, she was called back to the New York trading floor to take on global equities merchandising. She transformed this function into an innovative source of cross-cap-structure insights and collaborated closely with Global Investment Research to better commercialize and distinguish Goldman Sachs analysts and their ideas in an ultracompetitive marketplace. That same year, she was invited to become a partner at Goldman Sachs, a huge accomplishment, and one especially important to her as a woman: "At one point, I was the only woman partner in the equities division, globally, and I took seriously the opportunity to be a mentor and role model. She was also given the responsibility of heading the International Equities Sales and Trading Division, which comprised overseeing all the non-US equities desks for the North American institutional client base.

COO of Global Compliance at Goldman Sachs

Then Lisa was thrown a curve ball. "At the end of 2005, senior management asked me to take on a significant new leadership challenge amidst the intensifying regulatory environment—that of becoming the COO of the Global Compliance Division, with responsibilities later expanded to the legal and internal audit departments as well. I was truly shocked to be offered this opportunity; I was doing well in my role and didn't see it coming. I really had to think about whether I wanted to step away from the career and client relationships and reputation I had built to date, to make this big change. And I wondered, 'Could I even do this role?'" This was a pivotal moment for Lisa, and she looked to her lighthouse relationships for advice. "I suddenly got this insight that people tend to define themselves and their skills by the context in which they have used them to date. They don't stop and think. The skills that have made me successful in the current could also be useful in this new, totally different role. I had to learn to separate the skills I had from the way I had used them to that point and realized that this skill of client relationships, and the skill of running a business, could actually be very relevant in this COO role, even though the context—compliance, legal, and audit—was totally different. I decided to take the new role, and it turned out to be a fascinating experience." Lisa brought a revenue-business approach to these "nonrevenue" areas and came up with the goal of ensuring they became as highly regarded for how well they ran as businesses as they were for their deep subject-matter expertise. This was in 2006, at the very beginning of the period leading up to the financial crisis. Goldman Sachs became a bank holding company, and the control functions she managed were among the fastest-growing areas of the firm, requiring a rolled-up-sleeves focus on efficiency, creativity, technology, talent, and a global, business-enabling mindset. Lisa managed three divisions with global scope, a staff of over 1,300, and a multimillion-dollar technology budget.

Learning to Adapt and Earn Trust

After four and a half years in the COO role, Lisa was ready for her "next thing." Now that she had learned she was capable of dropping into completely new contexts and figuring out how to add value, she was very open-minded as to what her next role would be. She was asked to head brand marketing and digital strategy in the Executive Office. She said, "When I took the role, I was not even sure what the job description was. I just knew that there would be innovation and change involved and I would figure it out, and by that point, I was somewhat confident in my ability to be agile. What I did not expect, and what nobody expected, was that Goldman Sachs in particular would become a target at a time when Wall Street was really the source of a lot of blame for the financial crisis. As a result, a week and a half into the role, I ended up responsible for a brand in crisis. One important lesson I quickly learned is that a crisis creates opportunities. Sometimes it is hard to introduce change when everything is going well, but when you are in a situation where everything is called into question or the world seems to have turned upside down, that's when, oddly enough, people are open to new ideas and solutions." In this role she and her team launched Goldman's first corporate image advertising campaign, created digital and social channels (very new things at that time for any brand) and media partnerships, and redesigned the corporate website—all to convey "who we are, what we do, and why it matters," which helped Goldman Sachs be better understood by Main Street. "I could not have asked for a more fascinating and impactful role and team to work with."

Throughout her career at Goldman, Lisa had to learn how to quickly adapt as she continued to be dropped, out of the blue, into roles for which she had little experience: "As I have been in these roles where I am dropped into situations where I don't know anything, where I am surrounded by subject matter experts who know more than me and who know they know more than me, or where there is something that I need to do to drive change, I've found that, often, these roles can be very lonely. You are bringing in new ideas, and sometimes people do not want to change. From their perspective, they know more than you. How do you overcome the loneliness and a really profound sense of ownership of the risk of doing anything, assuming you can even make the change happen? I found ways to believe in the mission, to ask thoughtful questions, and show I could listen well, seek input, and see things from other perspectives so that I could win them over and get their buy-in. But believe me, there were many days where I just felt really on my own, even as part of a team. You have to have a lot of self-confidence and conviction and earn everyone's trust."

Shifting Priorities

In mid-2014, Lisa decided to leave Goldman Sachs. The sudden passing of her father after an accident the prior October influenced this decision. "Those personal moments make you pause. They make you think, 'Hold on, I need to slow down. I need to pick my head up.' The silver lining from that experience was that I hit pause … It is so easy to be consumed by the flow of being busy and feeling productive and making a contribution, but sometimes you have to pick your head up and make sure you are thinking about the whole portfolio of things and people in your life." Lisa was coming up on her twenty-year mark at Goldman Sachs and realized that her priorities had shifted from her all-consuming career she loved to try to be home for dinner every night with her teenage sons before they disappeared off to college. Lisa realized she had choices. Her financial success allowed her to make decisions that were not based on compensation. Although she received a lot of advice to stay in her job but work less and reduce her workload, she realized that for her, it was all-in or nothing, so she gathered up the courage to step away from her defining career at Goldman Sachs. She stayed on as an advisory director until end of January 2015 and then cut the cord.

Putting Her Experience to Work in New Ways

    Retirement is not the right word to describe Lisa's post-Goldman life. She began to meet with founders and advise start-ups during the day but made sure she would always be home in time for dinner with her sons. In the course of the many conversations she was having, she happened to come across an opportunity that interested her, and it made her realize how much she missed working. She became the chief marketing officer of Odyssey, a millennials-focused media platform, working for its twenty-seven-year-old founder for twelve months, an invaluable experience to better understand the start-up ecosystem. She also began serving on several public and private boards, which inspired her to create a community of women on corporate boards, Extraordinary Women on Boards, to discuss topics related to board excellence. She continues to love advising growth companies and putting her extensive and diverse business background and network to work to help them grow.

Philosophy

    As she reflects on her career, one of the most important realizations Lisa has had is "this insight that people tend to define themselves and their skills by the context in which they have used them to date. They define themselves by their past. So, when people are looking for new opportunities, they tend to go back to the old context or the old paths. I had to learn to separate the skills that I had from the way I had used them to that point, and I realized that this skill of client relationships could actually be relevant in different ways, or the skill of running a business or thinking about things this way or making presentations that way could be relevant in new contexts as well. So, my advice is this: people should not define themselves by what they've done before. They should look at the skills they've needed to succeed to date and find other contexts where those skills will be valuable, and then make a persuasive pitch and own their narrative."

Callie Haines

> **Lighthouses in Callie's Words**
>
> "My lighthouses are my two daughters. Even when I don't think I can continue to balance motherhood and my job successfully, I know they look up to me and love the fact that I work. They think I am strong, smart, and independent, and through their lens, I gain confidence and clarity as a businesswoman, but most importantly, as a mother and role model to them."

Early Years

Callie Haines, the senior vice president of the Asset Management Division at Brookfield, cherished the hours she spent working on various wood-working projects in her home's basement with her dad, while listening to Boston Celtics and the Red Sox games. Her father was employed in manufacturing, and he and her mother introduced her to the world of hard, hands-on work. She was studious in high school and, at home, was often caught hiding in her closet, reading books long after she was supposed to be asleep. This work ethic, combined with her love of hands-on problem solving, led her to Princeton in 1994 to major in civil engineering and architecture, a discipline not many women studied at that time.

Although her major did not require her to take business classes, she decided to take an economics class in her freshman year. It was a complete disaster. Because of this, business finance, initially, did not seem to be a promising career path for her. She was not completely sure what she wanted to do for a career, but she held close her memories of escape when she worked with her dad in their basement.

Civil Engineering

She reached out to the Turner Construction Company in 1998, right after she earned her degree, and was accepted as a project engineer. Her employment there helped her understand real estate from the ground up. Her first job at Turner consisted of basic entry-level tasks such as counting bricks and doing property surveys. On one survey, she came across a field of dead cows, which put a project on hold for one week.

Path to Success

The Turner Construction Company job marked the first time Callie felt she was a *girl*. During her childhood, the three varsity sports she played throughout high school and all the hours she spent wood-working with her dad led many people to regard her as a tomboy. She was in a leadership position from the beginning, but in a male-dominated field. She had to work hard to gain the respect of her colleagues, which helped her learn how to communicate with a wide variety of people. She worked with developers and laborers and had to understand what every employee brought to the table and how to put all of them in the best position to succeed. Technically, she learned a lot about the moving pieces of construction, such as how many different teams have to come together to make something happen.

MBA and Property Development

Being involved in construction and real estate necessitated enhancing her business background by earning an MBA degree. She took two years off, enrolling at the London Business School in 2003. She lived abroad while she had the chance to do so, which gave her a worldly outlook and an appreciation of different cultures and backgrounds, something she tries to integrate into her work. After graduating with an MBA degree, she started working for Brookfield Properties to build a development team. Brookfield is one of the largest real estate companies, with a portfolio of over $500 billion, including shopping malls, office towers, and more, across the globe.

As her career progressed, Callie struggled with being an introvert in roles that increasingly required her to be an extrovert in order to interact with wider groups and audiences. She just kept showing up and trying her hardest to communicate her message to a wide variety of employees. Three years into working at Brookfield, the financial crisis of 2008 took hold, and consequently, development was not a priority for Brookfield. At the same time, Callie was pregnant with her first child. She took a short leave of absence and when she returned, she moved to a new position.

Asset Management and Motherhood

Callie joined Brookfield's asset management team as their vice president. The team oversaw the entire USA initially, but as the company grew and transformed, the team focused on the New York and Boston regions with a range of real estate from harbor-front properties in Boston to one of the largest portfolios of commercial real estate in New York. At the time she was taking on this new set of large responsibilities, Callie was also continuing her life as a mom, which she found challenging.

Early on, she told her boss she wanted to quit because she found managing the job while being a mom too stressful. Her boss told her she was important, and they could make it work, convincing Callie to focus on becoming a strong role model for her two girls by continuing in the job. She doubled down on her two jobs: mother and, later, senior vice president, while trying her best to strike a balance.

Fighting for Gender Diversity

Throughout her life Callie has pushed herself very hard and has had to learn when to take a step back and focus on her family. She made family a priority and struck a balance: "It is a damn hard balance." Throughout her career she has always been the odd "man" out as a woman in a male-dominated field. She has not known anything else because she has never worked in an industry with an abundance of women. People sometimes assume she is an assistant or junior member of the team. She credits the flexibility, trust, and respect of her Brookfield colleagues for her success to date and has become a more vocal advocate for diversity.

Philosophy

Callie believes in workplace diversity. She champions women striving for success in all industries and works hard for women to be treated with equality. She also values the contribution that employees' experiences of other cultures can make in the workplace and encourages others to appreciate and experience cultural diversity, especially through traveling abroad.

Lisa Tepper

<u>**Lighthouses in Lisa's Words**</u>

"My lighthouse in my business career is Jay Fishman. Jay is the prior chairman and chief executive officer of The Travelers Companies. He unfortunately passed away in in 2016, far too early in his life. When I was initially offered a position to take on leadership responsibilities in New York and New Jersey, I respectfully declined the offer. Jay Fishman heard that I turned down this opportunity and he reached out to me. We had a very interesting conversation. It was clear that he respected my decision, but he said, 'Please hear me out. I see something in you that you may not see in yourself.' He was right. He described things about me that I didn't know were so impactful. These were authentic and genuine things about me. That conversation changed my life and I accepted the position. My lighthouse helped me be someone else's lighthouse.

Who was my personal board of directors? The connection here is W.O.M.E.N. In America. This group of women has been a support group for me personally and professionally. They are my lighthouse and they shine bright in everything that I do. I enjoy mentoring the talented group of rising leaders and receiving their mentorship as well."

Early Years

In high school, Lisa Tepper was a driven student, engaged with her community through volunteer work, and growing as a leader. She accepted many opportunities to lead clubs and serve on the student council. Upon graduation, she planned to continue her education with the goal of becoming an executive secretary. This was the only role Lisa was aware of as a career for a woman growing up in the 1970s. Lisa was determined that a secretarial role was her destiny until her mother told her that she should go to business school. Her mother was a stay-at-home mother who wanted Lisa to follow her passion to the right career: "My mom saw something in me that I did not see in myself. She gave me great guidance and introduced me to somebody who went to Katherine Gibbs College for professional secretaries. I did not see myself in that person, and that opened my eyes to other colleges."

Lisa eventually attended Siena College and pursued a career in insurance: "I got into insurance the way many people get into insurance. Insurance was nothing I ever thought of, but it was something that came my way." The summer before her freshman year of college she worked at a family-run insurance agency in her hometown of Troy, New York. "I knew that I wanted to be in business, so this was good experience. Being a lifeguard or a waitress would be more money and a better suntan, but I wanted the business experience." She continued to work at the insurance agency through the summers and holidays while she was in college. She became passionate about insurance, so she started taking insurance classes in college. She kept going back to the family-run insurance agency because she was passionate about providing clients with peace of mind when she worked on a solution to their problems. She enjoyed the fact that no two days were alike.

Path to Success

Lisa graduated from Siena College with a degree in marketing and business and accepted a position in the insurance industry as a marketing representative with Aetna Life and Casualty Company. As a representative of Aetna, she interacted with other insurance agencies, an experience that fed her love of relationship building and customer interaction. When she was promoted to the role of marketing superintendent, she learned what it meant to create a good team, to hire the right people for the job, and to embrace the feedback she was given. She worked to make the best professional environment she could for her team: "Rather than prioritizing financial goals and focusing on achieving the numbers, I would say, 'Let's analyze where we are today and plan for a future focused on the results we want to achieve.' I have always been a qualitative and quantitative person. When you are launching a new product or program, the qualitative outcomes will sustain the results. Focus on the action items you want to achieve versus how quickly you can get to the numbers."

A Career in Insurance

Lisa's career grew through a series of promotions at Aetna from marketing representative in New York to Aetna's home office in Hartford, Connecticut, where she helped to create a new division that focused on small businesses. In 1996, Aetna sold the property and liability insurance businesses to The Travelers Group, Inc. Lisa and her family relocated to Pennsylvania, where she led the integration of the small-business divisions. In 2004, St. Paul Companies and Travelers Property Casualty merged, and Lisa and her family moved again, this time to New Jersey, where Lisa led the downstate New York and New Jersey integration.

At Travelers, Lisa had a summer intern named Haytham Zohny. During their first discussions, Haytham told Lisa that he was not interested in a career in insurance. He wanted to go into investment banking, and he had taken the Travelers position for experience. Lisa told him, "Okay, Haytham, we will talk at the end of the summer." Haytham's objective was to diversify his experience through his internship, but he came to find the insurance industry fascinating. Today Haytham enjoys a successful career in insurance. He is a high performer and respected in the industry. "Just like my mother saw something in me," Lisa explains, "I saw something in Haytham."

Pursuing New Challenges and Championing Women in Business

Lisa's career transitioned from insurance carrier to insurance broker. She retired from Travelers and in 2017 joined Gallagher as the area executive vice president for the northeast region. Combining her insurance knowledge with her passion to help others, she provides insurance consultation, demystifying the process for her clients. Today, focused on her passion to support entrepreneurs and mentor women-led businesses, Lisa finds this the most fulfilling time in her career.

From her early student days, Lisa could not have charted the course of her career. She continually accepted new challenges, some of which, initially, she did not think she could overcome. The lessons of those experiences guided her throughout her journey. Lisa has focused on work she is passionate about, which includes helping others and networking. With little knowledge of what to expect, she attended a SheEO event (SheEO is a group of generous women who finance women innovators; see Vicki Saunders in this book). "The first thing that went through my mind," Lisa told me during our interview, "was 'I don't think I have ever been in a room filled with women that are 100 percent radically generous.' It is consistent generosity. It is generosity without judgment. It is being generous not only with your dollars but with your time, your passion, your heart, your words, your encouragement to others. I was 'all in' when I heard about radical generosity." Lisa is now a super activator for SheEO in New York City and participates in as many events as she can to meet and support this amazing group of women.

Philosophy

Lisa passionately believes in helping others and supporting women. She can see potential in people that others may have overlooked. She also values assessing the status quo for its development potential and working with existing conditions rather than setting goals without a firm base in current reality.

Managers & Analysts

Katherine Fischer

Early Years

Katherine Fischer's father ran his own wealth management firm in Wisconsin. As she watched him, Katherine began to take an interest in his line of work. Wealth management provides a variety of services to clients including insights on financial planning. Katherine liked the balance of interacting with clients and understanding how to map their goals and finances. She heard her father talk about the importance of understanding the psychology of his clients when he presented new ideas to them. This inspired Katherine's college focus and she graduated cum laude from Williams College with a BA in Economics and Psychology.

A Beginning in Management Consulting

Katherine graduated in 2008, when, due to the financial crisis, the banking and consulting firms that normally recruited college grads stopped recruiting. She adapted her search and began working as an associate consultant for Bain & Company, a management consulting firm. There she built the foundation of her approach to problem solving. Her job required her to do in-depth analysis, present her research, and make recommendations to a range of different clients. In addition to helping clients solve difficult problems, Katherine enjoyed interacting with individual clients, an aspect of her job she had wanted since observing her father in his practice.

Investing and Client Interaction

In 2010, Katherine took the aspects of her job she enjoyed the most, investments and client interaction, to the Gordon and Betty Moore Foundation, where she became an investment associate. She worked for Denise Strack, the foundation's chief investment officer (see Denise Strack in this book), focusing on asset allocation, liquidity, and cash planning, and helping various managers with due diligence work through an associate program. This wide portfolio of responsibilities gave her broad exposure to a lot of different asset categories because the foundation invested in public equities, fixed income, private equity, ventures, natural resources, and real estate. Katherine valued the knowledge and experience this broader exposure afforded her. Her analytical toolbox was greatly increased by the range of assets she worked with, but because she was working through an associate program, there was no career trajectory for her at that time.

Still, she had found her true passion for investing at the Gordon and Betty Moore Foundation and gained valuable skills and experience. She followed that passion to Sand Hill Global Advisors, a financial management company that advises individuals and foundations. While Katherine served as a portfolio manager for two years, she had her first daughter and completed the CFA program.

Path to Success

A headhunter approached Katherine about applying for a position as a portfolio manager at Hall Capital Partners, a financial management company with a minimum investment of $100 million. This would expose Katherine yet again to a different type of investing, including institutional capital, and would allow her to hone some of the techniques she had learned about endowment investing at the Gordon and Betty Moore Foundation.

Although she held the position of portfolio manager at Hall Capital, her role was more similar to that of a wealth manager (holistic client-centered planning and related services) rather than being solely focused on investment, as she was at Sand Hill. While Katherine enjoyed the holistic aspects of her job, most of the wealth management she dealt with centered on estate planning, wealth transference, and partnership structures. She began to miss working with clients confronting "real-life issues," which wealthier clients with assets in the billions were unlikely to face. And the long commute to her job and pending divorce only intensified her dissatisfaction with her work.

Katherine took a leave of absence to think about whether she was on the right career path. She returned to school, this time not for additional financial education but to add a new skill set: she took classes to get a license in marriage and family therapy (MFT).

Putting the Client First at Ensemble Capital

During Katherine's leave of absence, another headhunter approached her about working as a wealth manager for Ensemble Capital Management, a financial planning company in California. She was elated to be offered the opportunity to help clients with their general finances. The supportive and understanding culture of Ensemble Capital, created by President and CEO Sean Stannard-Stockton continues to inspire her to value and appreciate the work she is doing. She sets store by the fact that Ensemble puts the clients before anyone else, even if it means that sometimes the firm recommends products and services offered by another wealth management firm if they would suit the client better, an unusual step for a financial firm to take.

Katherine's days at Ensemble Capital are spent talking with clients, helping them with ongoing financial projects such as saving for college, retirement, tax planning, and thinking through insurance policies. This means many emails and calls to understand her clients' needs. Katherine describes the challenge, "Any person has a lot of options available to them, but there are different paths to get there. It is fulfilling to help someone figure out what they really want in their life, what is important to them, and what they want their life to look like— helping people figure that out and then making it happen with their finances."

In 2019, Katherine began studying for her certified financial planner (CFP) license to better help her clients achieve their individual financial goals. She enjoys learning about her clients in order to alleviate their financial stress and anxiety. Since finances are a source of stress for nearly everyone, Katherine knows her role as a wealth manager provides value and she works to make her clients feel comfortable with money. She enjoys being part therapist, part wealth manager for her clients. On the investing side, she focuses on the psychology of market participants. On the financial planning side, she focuses on understanding the psychology of her clients and what makes the most sense in terms of financial analysis versus psychology.

Her Sense of Social Responsibility

Right after college, Katherine and a college friend applied for a grant to start a nonprofit organization they named Reclaim Childhood: "Reclaim Childhood is a nonprofit organization that seeks to empower

Arab girls and women through sport and play. Reclaim Childhood provides sports leagues, clinics and summer camps to Arab girls ages eight to eighteen, and coaching clinics to adult women. The organization is run by young women for young women." Just as wealth management does, it broadens the view of what is possible for these young women and opens doors to other possibilities. Sports allow a growth mindset rather than a fixed mindset and offer a universally accessible way to do that.

Philosophy

Katherine is focused on helping her clients to understand financial concepts: "Educating clients is really important because if they know what they are invested in and know how we invest, when the market goes down, which it will, they have a lot more understanding and conviction in what they're holding and what they're doing and they are able to stay invested." In addition to her passion for putting clients' needs first, Katherine continues pushing to make the world a better place.

Erin Lash

Lighthouses in Erin's Words

"From early on my dad was the one that sparked the interest in investing. That was something we did together and bonded over, throughout high school and college. He has always been there as a support system for me. I could be incredibly nervous and anxious at midnight the night before a big test in college, and I could call him and he could provide that support and was always there as my champion and my cheerleader. He helped guide me to where I am today. I talk to my dad regularly whether that is over text or email. We live about two minutes from my parents. He had a career shift when I was in college, and now he does investing full-time. I would say he has been my lighthouse and that support system and that individual that I have always been able to look to when I have questions, concerns about what path I should ultimately choose. For that, I don't know what I would do without him in my life."

Early Years

Early in her life, Erin was inspired by her father and aunt's passion for investing. When she was ten years old, she bought shares of Blockbuster Video, her first stock. The company was a great growth story for the 1980s and 1990s, but then came the Internet and Netflix. "What I didn't get right was, obviously, Blockbuster's inability to update the business model to reflect changing technology/trends." This presaged her eventual professional focus on companies with sustainable competitive moats. All profitable businesses are challenged by competitors. Erin learned early that competitive threats can come from anywhere and only the companies with the strongest competitive advantage can survive.

Erin studied finance at Bradley University and graduated in 2001. After college, she began working for State Farm Insurance as an investment analyst. She started her career as a generalist, covering sectors ranging from transportation to retail companies, and she credits her early experience across a wide range of companies with increasing her thirst for knowledge. Many analysts start out by covering a single economic sector, such as utilities or technology, and they dive deep into that one sector. By starting as a generalist, Erin observed sector-specific behaviors, which helped her, later on, to collaborate with colleagues in other sectors and see how different sectors of the economy interacted with each other. Her early Blockbuster experience of observing competition at work in multiple sectors of the economy reinforced her awareness that the number of potential external factors that can impact a company are unlimited. During her employment at State Farm, she worked toward her MBA in Finance and Accounting in the weekend program at the University of Chicago Booth Business School, and she also went on to complete the CFA program.

Path to Success

These experiences helped Erin build a base of knowledge that she carried with her to Morningstar, a financial services company: "I would say the long-term fundamental analysis that was core at State Farm was very much in line with how Morningstar thinks about investing, which made the transition fairly seamless." Erin started at

Morningstar in 2006, on the financials team. The year 2007 was tumultuous, especially for financial companies. After working there for eighteen months, Erin witnessed another major disruption firsthand: most of the financial companies she had originally covered had gone bankrupt.

Morningstar

In 2008, Erin moved to Morningstar's consumer sector team, which covers many household names and products such as McCormick Spice, Procter & Gamble (Tide, Pampers), Hershey's, and so on. The consumer sector is a particularly interesting one for many investors for several reasons. In the USA, consumers account for roughly two-thirds of GDP spending,[10] and due to the day-to-day use of many of the products, the companies that make them tend to have more stable earnings over time. After years of being an analyst for Morningstar, a job she felt passionate about, Erin was promoted in 2016 to the position of director of consumer equity research.

Erin was born for an analyst position. She is notorious for her ability to push herself and go deeper into a company she is researching. In the past, she did not form an opinion until she knew everything about every aspect of a company. Through her many interviews with employees of the companies she researched, she learned to put more weight behind simple but critical questions, allowing her to uncover insights on struggles within a company and its management. Over time, she learned to have confidence in the work she did without having to know absolutely everything about a company, but she continues to seek answers to her many questions.

What makes her passionate about her job is more than her desire to learn; she believes strongly in the values of Morningstar: "I love our long-term focus, and being able to assess near-term events through the lens of the long term is something that aligns with my own personal investment style. I like the collaboration, both within our team but also across other sector teams and other areas of the department. I feel that it is this collaboration and willingness to vet or challenge ideas internally that enables the quality of our research to continue to improve."

Finding Her Voice

As Erin moved into the director role at Morningstar, she noticed that she was the only female director in the North American sector. However, she doesn't let that discourage her: "I am often the only female in a meeting, but I don't try to see it that way. I do feel that I bring a different perspective, and maybe it is partly because I am a female, and maybe it is partly because I am who I am. But I have made sure that even when I am the only female, it doesn't mean that I am not speaking up. I do voice my opinions. If you think of investing and being an analyst, my job is, essentially, to have an opinion, and I joke that I get paid to have an opinion. Obviously, my opinion needs to be well founded and substantiated, and it is not something I take lightly … I don't let that limit the contribution that I try to make in our group, our department, and our company as a whole just because I am a female."

Erin pushes herself in her field regardless of her surroundings. However, she is very aware of the gender diversity problem and works to change it: "Having diversity just for the sake of it isn't necessarily the right vein. It is making sure that you are surrounded by quality individuals that can contribute and have different opinions."

Erin's zest for her subject is evident in her love for puns. Erin's countless articles on Morningstar elicit a smile. Listed below are some of her favorite punny titles:

- Kraft Heinz Brews Profits, but We Can't 'Ketchup' to the Valuation.
- Souring Sales Trends Don't Hurt Hershey's Sweet Wide Moat.
- Long-Term Investors Should Warm to Campbell's Chilled Valuation.

Keeping Abreast of Consumer Trends

Just as Erin experienced disruptions in her early Blockbuster investment as a ten-year-old and the financial crisis as she began her career, she has also experienced another set of disruptions in her work, this time in consumer staples. For many decades, consumer staples were considered the most resistant to change, as brands such as Kellogg's, Kraft, Campbell's Soup, and Coca Cola dominated for decade after decade. Now, many long-lived brands are under threat due to changing consumer tastes, which limit the growth of these companies and impact their competitive moats.

Erin's work as an analyst for Morningstar has been following these trends and analyzing the implications for investors. On the competitive moat side, the situation for companies has become more challenged because there are no switching costs for consumers who stop drinking the beverage of one company and start drinking the beverage of another. This limits the branded companies' ability to raise prices. Erin identifies areas of strength for companies in this way: "Products that afford consumers added convenience, and/or those with a health and wellness bent (including organics and snacking) have seen increased demand."

As an example of a company that navigated the current challenges well, Erin points to McCormick Spice, maker of the brands Zatarain's, Lawry's, Old Bay Seasoning, French's, Frank's Red Hot, and more. In an interview I had with Erin in 2018, she commented that as many brands struggled to grow, "McCormick again bucked the trend of stagnant sales plaguing industry operators, boasting a 2.7 percent organic top-line increase in its recently reported second quarter (primarily the result of higher volumes). We view this uptick even more favorably, given it came on top of 4.5 percent growth a year ago. Management attributed this to distribution wins, particularly on its home turf, for its recently acquired French's and Frank's line-ups. We think this speaks to the entrenched edge McCormick has amassed with leading retailers. In our view, this standing creates a virtuous cycle, starting with scale, affording manufacturers a mutually beneficial relationship with retailers, through which the vendor is an important retail partner, developing sales strategies to maximize volumes and retailers' margins while also prioritizing its own brands. As such, while intense competitive pressure (from other branded operators, small niche peers that have proved more agile in responding to evolving consumer trends and lower-priced private-label fare) is likely to persist, we believe McCormick will be able to withstand these challenges longer-term because of its solid competitive positioning."

Erin's work highlighted a key bit of counterintuitive information in analyzing McCormick Spice. Most of the older branded companies focused on rigorously cutting costs, driving out as many inefficiencies as they could find. This made the current year and short-term-projected profitability numbers look better to investors. However, cutting costs also limited the companies' abilities to invest in their own brands and innovate for the long term. McCormick did the opposite, and increased brand spending and acquired new brands such as Frank's Red Hot and French's, which resonated with consumers. Erin's timely analysis concluded that this created a mutually beneficial relationship for McCormick and its retail customers. While many branded food companies have seen their moats erode over time, as Blockbuster did, McCormick, by reinvesting in its core, has defended its portfolio of leading brands.

Philosophy

Erin strives to offer well-founded and substantiated opinions and advocates for workplace diversity with a focus on highly qualified people from a wide range of backgrounds.

Jenn Cole

Lighthouses in Jenn's Words

"I was incredibly shy as a teenager. How shy? We had to memorize a soliloquy for my ninth-grade English class. We didn't have to explain the soliloquy, just read it out loud. It seemed so easy, but I was terrified. I did not look up from the podium once. In fact, I still remember the pattern of the wood grain and the hole someone had carved into it. Moving to a new high school two weeks before I turned sixteen was not exactly my dream come true. Don't get me wrong. I wasn't completely miserable, but I was close. Lucky for me, Ann-Marie Schell, a student in my second-period class, invited me to eat lunch with her and her friends on my first day. She told me later that she remembered her first day at a new school and she didn't want me to sit alone on my first day. I continued to sit with this group over the next two weeks.

On my birthday, another student, Nia Pleasants, gave me a hand-written birthday card. I couldn't believe it. It was so thoughtful. She had wanted to get me balloons but said she didn't think I'd like the extra attention. She was right.

These people were more than kind; they were paying attention to the people around them in a more detailed, thoughtful way. It made an impact. Nia and I have been close friends since then. In those fifteen years, she has taught me a lot about being thoughtful in every interaction and task. It is a value I have been proud to adopt. She is my lighthouse."

Early Years

When Jenn started at the University of Mary Washington, she intended to create her own architecture major by combining her interests in historic preservation, art history, and mathematics. She thought that major would be the perfect intersection of her aptitude for math and her growing love for buildings. However, after failing to be placed in a key art history class and realizing the difficult nature of the architecture job market, Jenn was back to square one: clueless about what she wanted to do. It was then that her college calculus professor, Dr. Chiang, asked her to meet with him.

Trying to sort through her confusion on where to go next, Jenn remembered she had always enjoyed math. Dr. Chiang helped her understand the payoffs of majoring in math. Within one hour of meeting with Dr. Chiang, she declared the major she wanted to pursue, and she had a new advisor.

However, once she graduated in 2006 with a bachelor's degree in mathematics, she again did not know what to do. As a mathematics graduate, she felt she only had two options: attend graduate school, or pursue a career in teaching, neither of which appealed to her very much. All she could think was "What would I pursue in graduate school, and how would I possibly pay for it? How could I be responsible for teaching students something as fundamental as math? What if I screwed it up and hundreds of students failed because of me?"

Path to Success

Jenn decided to post her resume online and quickly got an invitation to interview next day for a temporary position as a catastrophe (CAT) management analyst. Jenn thought the job title was interesting and the company, Markel Insurance, seemed a promising one to start her career with. "Little did I know, when I accepted the temp position, that I was about to embark on a challenging and rewarding career path at an exceptional organization." Jenn did not plan to pursue a career in insurance as her dad had done for over twenty years.

The Markel Style

Markel began its business in 1930, insuring municipal jitney buses. Over the decades, it has expanded into many different specialty insurance areas, focusing on hard-to-insure lines that many big insurance companies shy away from. The specialty areas include insuring the red slippers that Judy Garland wore in the *Wizard of Oz* movie, collectible cars, martial arts schools, motorsports, and more. Since 2005, Markel has expanded its operations into noninsurance businesses that run the gamut from dredging companies to industrial plants to Brahmin handbags and Belgian waffle makers.

Being a CAT analyst taught Jenn the importance of meaningful working relationships. Since Markel is a diverse financial holding company of many niche markets, it is not unusual for employees to have daily interactions with each other across the range of different fields within the company in order to better understand the "product lines and complexities which need to be properly quantified." Jenn also finds that her work is meaningful and relevant when she thinks about its big picture impact. "When you feel your work is valued, you tend to be more thoughtful in your execution. To me, thoughtfulness includes more than just being kind. The main idea here is tackling issues, tasks, interactions, and more, with a sense of purpose, attention to detail, and care. The feedback received for a thoughtful gesture or a thoughtfully created project are rewarding for both parties."

Her original temp position turned into a six-year position, but in 2012, Jenn took on the role of senior CAT analyst. The Markel style has supported and encouraged Jenn in her career: "At Markel we hold the individual's right to self-determination in the highest light, providing an atmosphere in which people can reach their personal potential. Being results-oriented, we are willing to put aside individual concerns in the spirit of teamwork to achieve success."[11] The "Markel Style" statement is posted prominently on the company's website, throughout the offices, and on many desks, and Jenn feels that it has encouraged her to think out of the box and turn to other resources and colleagues to benefit from their knowledge and skill sets.

In 2014, Jenn was promoted to the position of supervisor of CAT management. Shortly after, her department went through a five-month period short of staff, resulting in a continuous stream of projects that her three-person team had to work tirelessly to complete. Since this was her first year as supervisor, she felt pressured to push her team to complete every task handed to them, which meant she had to stay after-hours every night and on weekends. "I cried from exhaustion on more than one occasion. Every morning I rallied myself and worked to stay on top of tasks for our team. The team worked hard and I'm very proud of what we were able to accomplish."

Fighting Prejudice

Although the Markel style has created a supportive community for Jenn, being in a male-dominated field has posed some problems. Early on when her male colleagues spoke over her or reiterated her points, she found it difficult to not take it personally. It was particularly difficult to keep my cool when an outside vendor consistently stopped our meeting to ask if a male colleague or my male manager could please join the meeting even after he had been told that I was the primary expert on the topic. This vendor rep was, thankfully, released from the project when I notified a male colleague about his behavior."

Empowering leaders and colleagues in her career and field have helped her learn how to handle herself in these difficult situations and how to be strong and persevere. Because of those experiences and her positive lighthouses, she is equipped to present her ideas clearly and speak up for herself and others when she needs to.

Philosophy

Jenn strives to take a deeply thoughtful approach to her work and to her relationships, to share her ideas and learn from others, and to empower others along the way.

Jen Likander

Lighthouses in Jen's Words

"As I reflect on my current journey and position, I could list several people that I would consider to be my "lighthouse." I also don't think you have to only have one person at a time to guide you through situations. I believe that there are several people who guide me, and I rely on all of them equally, but at different times and for different situations. I would consider my most recent manager to be a career lighthouse for me. She has had a very successful career in insurance, and her knowledge, determination, and professionalism have helped, and are helping, to "light" the way of my career. I have full trust in her decisions and leadership. As I've moved into a new position, she has helped to direct me and guide me on my path forward.

Two other people I would consider as lighthouses for me are two colleagues of mine. Both are in separate departments and areas of the company. They are both people that I admire for their success and work ethic. They both have been successful in their careers, but they have had very different paths in their journeys. Having people in my network but outside my department helps to provide different perspectives and thoughts that I often don't consider. They have different opinions than I do, but I know, when I call them, they give me the most unbiased, completely honest feedback that helps to mold some of the decisions I've made. Lighthouses, networks, and mentors are essential to setting up a trusted inner circle."

Early Years

Jen Likander fell into insurance, as many do. Her family and friends viewed insurance as a "necessary evil" industry of people who did cold calls and door sales, attempting to overcharge customers, so her decision to pursue a career in that industry was a shock to them and to her. The only experience she and her family ever had with insurance was paying their annual insurance bills.

When she started at Indiana State University, Jen was lost. "My university was known for its teaching and nursing school. I wanted to do neither of those. I was not confident that I even picked the right school, much less thinking I would find a major and career I would enjoy."

Jen struggled to find a subject she enjoyed. She tried accounting, marketing, IT, and general business classes, but none of them really fit her. During her junior year, she was panicking because she had not yet declared a major and needed another class for her fall schedule. "With a lot of decisions to be made, and little direction about where to head, I made an appointment with my advisor to talk about options and where I should be considering."

Her advisor encouraged her to take her class on general insurance that semester, and they would continue the search for the best major for Jen. Although Jen was nervous and hesitant, she signed up. That class broadened her entire perspective on business and insurance. "Realizing how vital insurance was to the economy, to health, and to overall general operations, I finally understood how many possibilities insurance created." Within three weeks of going to the class, Jen declared her major, and in 2008, she graduated with a BS in Insurance and Risk Management. This revelation and leap of faith started a passion for risk management and insurance that has grown for twelve years.

Path to Success

In June 2008, Jen started a position as an underwriter at Markel, an insurance company based in Virginia (see Jenn Cole in this book).. She learned the fundamentals of insurance and risk management and during the six years she worked as an underwriter, she sat next to different people in her field. This allowed her to understand and appreciate the perspectives of others and learn that there is more than one way to get to the right answer. "Listen to all thoughts and opinions because there are always two sides to a story or situation. Do your research and know your facts. It's easy to hear something and assume something is wrong or not working correctly and turn it into a bigger issue." She learned to dig into the information given to her and not take it at face value.

Her say-yes attitude to opportunities also helped her change her initial stance and enhance her career.

When she was promoted to the position of senior underwriter in September 2014, she jumped at the opportunity to advance her career while remaining in the same empowering environment. Even after working at Markel for over twelve years, Jen finds the company continues to push her to reach her full potential, and she is one of the "newer" underwriters, which shows the true effect of the Markel style (its culture). "Knowing there is a built-in culture that helps to model my career and feel supported is empowering." This culture has helped her in many ways, as reflected in the following line in the "Markel Style" statement: "We are encouraged to look for a better way to do things ... to challenge management."[12] This makes Jen feel she is part of a supportive community working to make a difference in Markel and in insurance.

She has always been encouraged to share her ideas and look for better ways to do things.

Learning Creates Opportunities

When a program Jen handled was discontinued, her team had to merge with another team, which presented substantial learning-curve struggles including coping with new systems, programs, and processes. However difficult that might have been, it created many opportunities for her to move into the new position of senior commercial underwriter. "After getting through the initial process of new, I realized how exciting the additional programs were, as it created a chance for me to learn and expand my skill set that I may not have had. It took me moving into a new position to help enforce what I've always believed in: you need to take chances and trust in those decisions." The substantial amount of knowledge she acquired in this new position she believes will be crucial for other aspects of her career.

A Supportive Environment

The supportive community fostered by the Markel style increases the empowerment of women in a male-dominated field. Throughout her career at Markel, Jen's managers have predominantly been women: "I have been fortunate in my career to work in a department that has strong, empowering female leadership. Because I have admired and learned from all of them, and learned from how they have handled themselves, I have never felt that women cannot be as successful as men in the insurance industry. I have known others who have not been nearly as fortunate as I have been in regards to influential women in their careers, and I always hope they have an equally influential team of women in their lives. The women in my department have been my peers, managers, friends, but most importantly, they have been my role models. I strive to model my attitude, thoughts, and career after their paths."

This does not mean she has not felt intimidated as a woman in insurance. During one of her first client visits, she was the only woman in the meeting, a typical situation in her early years that challenged her efforts to establish meaningful relationships with her clients. She solved this problem by creating conversation starters to fill uncomfortable gaps in the conversation.

Philosophy

Jen believes in sharing ideas, learning from others, continually doing due diligence and looking for better ways to do things, taking calculated risks, and having the self-confidence to stand by one's decisions.

Champions of Socially Responsible Investing

Alyce Lomax

Lighthouses in Alyce's Words

"I would say a lot of my current and former Motley Fool colleagues are lighthouses, but if I have to pick one person, it would be my mom. She has always believed in me and has been so proud of my accomplishments but also at times has steered me in ways that I might not have gone on my own. Granted, I don't always do what she thinks I should—me interviewing at start-ups in people's houses used to freak her out when I was in my twenties. That whole concept was so new back then and older generations were used to people working for one company all their lives and then retiring with a pension. Still, she is always my biggest cheerleader and defender and at times, makes me step back and think of things in a different way."

Early Years

From 1988 until 1992, Alyce attended St. Mary's College of Maryland, where she majored in language and literature. Although that was a formative experience that molded much of her life, for personal reasons, she withdrew from college just short of an official degree. She had always dreamed of being a writer, but during that time, jobs for aspiring writers and even college graduates were few and far between, so she decided it was unrealistic to wait for the perfect day job. She took a job as a typist at a subcontractor to the Securities and Exchange Commission. She advanced steadily within the organization, but as the Internet became more prominent, Alyce realized she wanted to take her experience as an English major and use it for a job in the business and

financial information field. Shortly after, she found a job at Comtex
News Network in its Top News Summaries Division. She learned
firsthand of the limitless possibilities of the Internet such as constant
access to real-time news. Her job exposed her to many aspects of
journalism and finance in the early dot-com days that continued to
intrigue her and led to her next job.

Although Alyce was continuously exposed to the stock market
through her job at Comtex, she did not buy her first stock until the mid to
late nineties, during the dot-com bubble. Throughout her life, she has
been an avid reader of The Motley Fool and followed that service
closely, but she fell victim to the excitement of the dot-com bubble and
learned some valuable lessons when she bought shares in some
unsuccessful technology companies. Not all her investments were bad,
though. She also was an early shareholder of Amazon and XM Satellite
Radio. These investments could have paid off in the long haul, but Alyce
was laid off from her job when the dot-com bubble burst and had to sell
her shares in all of her stocks. Yet again, she struggled to find a job that
fit her.

Path to Success
In the mid-90s, Alyce decided that she wanted to work for The
Motley Fool. She interviewed three times for different positions at The
Fool: "I think giving up too easily on things you want is a mistake, and
trying again, sometimes repeatedly, can really pay off." It did pay off
because in 2003 she was hired as a writer and analyst at The Fool. The
Shakespearean inspiration behind its name (it comes from the play *As
You Like It*) most attracted Alyce to the company. A *fool* in medieval

times was a court jester, the only member of the king's court who could be brutally honest with the king without getting his head chopped off. The Motley Fool is "dedicated to educating, amusing, and enriching individuals in search of the truth." She also found her English major, along with the company's supportive atmosphere, helped her be a successful employee: "It seemed like a natural place for someone like me to want to be."

Socially Responsible Investing

The critical thinking strategies she learned in college became important to her, as an analyst. She found there are lots of "unreliable narrators and narratives" in the industry, and an important part of investing is to ferret out the difference between the "good" and the "too good to be true." Throughout her career at The Fool, Alyce has become a specialist in SRI. She worked on The Motley Fool's Real-Money Portfolio project to show investors that social responsibility with investing does not have to come at the cost of high returns.

When Alyce began to focus on SRI about ten or so years ago, it was still a very small niche in the investing industry, with only a handful of funds specializing in the combination of aligning values with investments. Since her early days of writing about SRI, it has flourished alongside environmental, social, and governance (ESG) investing to become a major growth area in the investing community.

True investors—as opposed to traders—focus on the long term. Over the long haul, how a company affects the environment, society, and the world matters just as much as profits. In other words, investors do not have to choose between a great investment and a company that makes them feel good. As Alyce explains, "I don't believe investors have to sacrifice! These days, there are more and more companies that are doing great work in making their businesses more sustainable, stakeholder-centric, and so forth. The range of choices we can make of companies to invest in while keeping our values in mind is expanding. Of course, it also helps to be a patient, long-term investor buying shares of high-quality, well-managed companies—and often, those kinds of companies are stakeholder-centric."

Increasingly, younger investors factor social responsibility into their valuations of companies, but there are other investors who do not want to mix personal values with money making. Alyce has therefore made it her mission to educate investors on SRI: "Let's not forget the SRI integration element involves mitigating risk: if a company that's been hurting stakeholders in the blind, irresponsible pursuit of short-term shareholder value blows up and the stock collapses, well, they've lost money. People don't always realize SRI is a way to try to avoid downside risk. For many investors to be able to fully sleep at night, they'd want to stick to SRI portfolios or companies."

Most recently, Alyce and John Rotonti published an ESG Investing Framework that seeks to combine the search for great returns and investing for the greater good. Their ESG Compounder checklist looks for companies that score seven or better on ten checklist items (see Appendix A for details).

Starbucks and Costco

Asked for some examples of where both social responsibility and profitability coincide, Alyce has ready examples, "Starbucks and Costco are two of my favorite examples right off the top of my head, particularly in the employee treatment area, and long-time shareholders most certainly can't complain about how well those stocks have performed over the course of years."

Remember the root of the word *investing* means "to clothe." SRI is a really awesome, green cloak that investors can wear proudly, knowing they are positively impacting the future. You choose what you want to wear, and you choose what future you are going to invest in.

Philosophy

During her time at The Fool, Alyce has led the way in SRI in the industry. She has been able to follow her dream of being an impactful writer.

Shilpa Andalkar

> **Lighthouses in Shilpa's Words**
>
> "I couldn't land on any person. I landed on gut and intuition. I feel like that has been my strongest lighthouse, but there is a lot I need to do to be able to listen to it. When I get out of my own way, I can actually listen to it."

Early Years

As a child, Shilpa's immigrant family pushed her towards investing, but she was never all that interested in the field until she went to college. Shilpa graduated from the University of California San Diego with a BS in Management Science. Throughout her life, Shilpa was sensitive to the welfare of her surroundings, leading to an interest in protecting the environment. She followed this interest after graduation, serving as a manager at the California League of Conservation Voters, a nonprofit organization that focused on political action for the environment. During her time at the nonprofit, Shilpa watched the animated documentary titled *The Story of Stuff* by Annie Leonard and became alarmed by the idea of a linear economy with finite resources, something never discussed in her economics studies. After working at the league for six and a half years, she left in 2012 to seek alternative ways to educate people about environmental and social issues.

She had invested in a 401k because she knew it was the responsible long-term thing to do, but it wasn't until she became interested in other "levers" beyond the nonprofit sector to educate people about such issues as clean air and water, healthy food, and human capital that she turned to investing as a career.

Shilpa came across the idea of impact investing and began working at HIP Investor, becoming the senior vice president of the Impact Investment Advisory Services Division. Although she dealt with the financial profile of investments, her main responsibility was to bring to light a stock or bond issuer's nonfinancial metrics. She produced HIP Investor's environmental, social, governance (ESG; see Appendix A for a description) scores that measured the nonfinancial ESG aspects of a company. The rating was made up of the quantitative outcome-related metrics of a corporation such as energy and water efficiency, board diversity, injury incidents, employee benefits, and retention rates.

During her time at HIP, Shilpa enjoyed working one-on-one with clients because it gave her a chance to see, firsthand, the response to her work. She was able to continue to do this when she joined Brio Financial Group as an associate financial advisor in 2015.

Path to Success

Shilpa's new position dealt with more than investments: she enjoyed the holistic aspect of a career in wealth management. Another career move brought her to the investment management firm of Ensemble Capital Management (see also Katherine Fischer in this book) in California. As a wealth manager, Shilpa is the central facilitator of financial conversations, so she takes time to carefully understand each client's situation and find ways to deliver the best investments for all clients, based on their goals and situation.

Educating Clients in Wealth Management

Wealth management allows Shilpa to grow and get better at her job because every day is different. She works to help her clients set their unique goals and analyze the path to get there. She educates them on the impossibility of controlling the market, which helps them to avoid letting short-term fluctuations erase their long-term progress toward their goals. And she continues to help her clients understand the financial and nonfinancial strengths of the companies they invest in. She credits her gender with greatly contributing to her success as a wealth manager. She believes that a kind and caring face helps when discussing financial planning trade-offs and decisions, and she tries to offer an informed take on each client's situation and risks.

Hewlett Packard conducted a study on the confidence levels of male and female job applicants.[13] The study found that most women have to be 100 percent confident they have *all* the qualifications whereas men will apply if they only meet 60 percent of qualifications. Throughout her finance career, Shilpa was heavily affected by not feeling ready to take the next step or by feeling that she did not belong: "My thorn is overanalyzing whereas with a male investor it appears that there is less doubt. The other element of never feeling ready is knowing when it is time to take the next step forward or make a change. I had a ton of challenges throughout my career, questioning what I "should" be doing. Working with certain personalities was hard, but more so, quieting my internal dialogue when walking a path without a clear outline. It takes time to see the results of certain decisions and having patience with that process." Shilpa hopes that women considering a career in finance, some of whom may have a different background from most of those working in finance, or who don't see others like themselves in finance, know that they, too, can belong in the financial space and have something important to offer.

Philosophy

Throughout her life, Shilpa Andalkar has been passionate about environmental and food system issues. She has volunteered for many causes. Her first job out of college was working for a nonprofit that specializes in political action for the environment. Through her career in finance, she realizes both nonprofit and for-profit business can influence broader change and better well-being for people and the planet.

Students

Monsoon Pabrai

Lighthouses in Monsoon's Words

"My lighthouse would be knowing when I am not happy, finding my purpose. When you are not having fun, something is wrong. My family is my lighthouse. They helped me to realize I was not happy and try something else."

Early Years

Monsoon Pabrai, is like her name: she prevails with force. She was born into the world of finance. Her father, fund manager Mohnish Pabrai, tried to encourage Monsoon and her sister to be as fascinated with investing as he is. She graduated from the University of California Berkeley in 2017, but don't let her short career fool you. Monsoon is the current marketing and community lead at Coral Labs, a start-up company. Prior to working at Coral Labs, she was an investment analyst intern at the UCLA Foundation and worked as a research analyst for Dalton Investments.

During dinner, if her father was excited about a recent investment, he would break it down for Monsoon and her sister. She became curious and wanted to invest on her own. In 2003, her father encouraged her and her sister to buy their first stock: "What is one company you love, and you think will be around for a long time?" Monsoon and her sister thought about companies they grew up with and knew well, and after thoughtful analyses, they invested in Target and Disney. They thought that these companies could sustain long-term growth and be successful over the long haul.

About ten years later, after seeing that Warren Buffett's Berkshire Hathaway had bought shares in Visa, Monsoon became a shareholder of Mastercard because of the company's growth, scale, and the way it moved with the economy: "I think it is worth copying ideas from people you look up to." She started with a question, "How does Visa make money?" And then she dug into the company. When Monsoon noticed that Visa was expensive, especially compared to Mastercard, she decided to buy shares in Mastercard "because I thought it was the same, exact thing as Visa." During her research, she found out that Mastercard had almost 100 percent gross profit per new customer, which she understood as an uncommon ideal.

Monsoon forgot about her shares in Mastercard until she became interested in joining clubs at UC Berkeley. When she found an investment club she wanted to join, she pitched Mastercard to the club's interview panel—and she was in! "I told them I picked Mastercard, and that they had close to 100 percent gross profits on new users, really no cost to add users. The club liked what I pitched and put me in the club."

University of California, Berkeley

Starting out at UC Berkeley, Monsoon majored in economics, but then she received advice "to be the most interesting version of herself." She changed her major to political science because of the reading, writing, and global perspectives. In polisci she could read and write about anything from writing a forty-page paper on the Two Chinas policy or on a crime that happened against people of her faith in India. She eventually extended her love of the research part of political science to the detailed corporate research she had to do as an investor: "It is almost like a dentist performing a root canal when I study businesses."

Becoming an Analyst

Despite her family background and love of research, Monsoon did not have any initial interest in becoming a fund manager like her father: "I couldn't align myself with giving profits to already-wealthy people. I think the Berkeley girl in me had a tough internal struggle." Monsoon interned as an analyst for the university endowment during the summers of in her sophomore and junior years. She became intrigued by the idea of managing investments for nonprofits and raising and growing money for good as a way to put her analytical and research skills to work for a wider purpose. "The beneficiary [of the endowment] was a financial aid student. Every year the endowment pays out 5 percent, and so the larger the endowment grew, the more they could pay out." She loved the fact that her work could benefit students who might otherwise not be able to attend college.

Path to Success

Monsoon's experience at the endowment fund prompted her to ask her boss for a job, but he encouraged her to practice equity research. She mailed her resume and a stock write-up to four hundred companies for entry-level equity-research positions. Out of four hundred applications, she was invited to four interviews but received no job offers. She persisted. In her second attempt, she sent out 750 applications. This time she received a "thanks but no thanks" response rate of about 10 percent and seven invitations to interviews, which led to two job offers. One was on the East Coast at a female-owned ESG firm. The other was to work on a $20 million India fund at a $4 billion Asia-focused value shop. It was a chance to connect with her Indian heritage while exploring her love for value, which her father, as a value investor, had instilled in her. She picked the offer to work on investing in Indian companies at Dalton Investments in Los Angeles.

India is a market going through enormous changes. As with other emerging markets, the rules, standards, and processes in India vary greatly from investing in the USA and the developed world.

Monsoon spent six months living in Mumbai, India, so she could be engaged with the culture there. Then she moved back to California to work with Dalton's global team. This was when she learned how to formally research companies, track companies, tune into earnings calls, keep up with the news, and maintain a list of companies that Dalton was interested in. "We were all generalists, looking for great companies at a good price. It was pretty diversified, and the final selection would naturally be diversified."

Monsoon learned a lot about corruption through her dealings with the Indian market. "Some of these guys [running Indian companies] would give themselves an annual salary of $10,000 a year, and their capex was in the millions. What are you paying for and why? Were they buying businesses and growing their businesses to benefit the shareholder or themselves and their friends? Many of the companies in India—the insiders owned almost 70 percent of the stock and then their friends would help them control up to 90 percent of the company. Alignment of interest plays a big part in Asian stock selection."

During our conversation in the summer of 2019, Monsoon told me, "I parted with Dalton after two years, with big personal questions. The first was to learn how to scale a business personally and the second was to see if I could run my own fund the way Jamie Rosenwald at Dalton and my father do."

Branching Out from Business Management to Entrepreneurship

Monsoon left Dalton Investments to take an unpaid internship at a start-up. She mailed out 1,000 resumes to different start-ups and got fourteen interviews. "The biggest challenge is getting your foot in the door, sending out all the letters. I think I will do that the rest of my life. It's a great way to be taken seriously at a young age." She decided to join a start-up company that makes a device to paint nails, simplifying and automating a normal trip to the nail salon. Monsoon works on business development at the company: how to bring in new customers, how to market the device, who the company's ideal customer is, and how to price the product. In school and at Dalton, Monsoon honed her research and analytical skills to study other companies for investment purposes. Now she is using those same skills to try to grow a company from scratch.

Monsoon advises job applicants to always have a good stock pitch. What worked for her in joining college clubs can also work in job searches. Some of the less well-known companies can be great opportunities and allow job applicants to showcase their analytical depth and next-level thinking. For example, Monsoon loved shopping at Dillard's, a clothing store based in the South. When she saw that David Einhorn (founder and president of the hedge fund Greenlight Capital) had bought shares in Dillard's, she wondered what David Einhorn knew about the place she shopped at. His purchase of shares did not make sense to her, so she did her research and learned that Dillard's owned valuable real estate: "It was kind of a real estate investment trust (REIT) company, not just a retail store. It was interesting, different, and made a lot of sense to me. It was a great pitch to send out to 750 fund managers.

Some of them had owned it before, or still owned it, and loved chatting with me, offline, about the company."

She also has learned that having a general knowledge of politics, and an awareness of market and cultural trends indicate a sense of engagement that can help win a job.

Philosophy

It has not all been perfect for this young woman in the workplace: "There are negative people out there who undermine you and try to make you feel small. I had a family friend who asked me to my face, 'How do they take you seriously?'" Rather than hurting her or making her doubt her choices, this remark reminded Monsoon that she mails her letters out and hustles the way she does "to be taken seriously. You just go on. Especially as a woman, people may see you as weak, dainty, and unintelligent. But you just keep reminding yourself about who you are, what you are doing, and your purpose on this planet."

Michelle Sindhunirmala

Lighthouses in Michelle's Words

"It's hard to name one lighthouse, but I would have to say my top three are: Mary Callahan Erdoes, Dottie Herman, and Barbara Corcoran. They are all self-made women and very successful in their industries. Dottie Herman created a real estate empire that is currently the third largest in the USA. Barbara Corcoran used to be a waitress and had straight Ds in high school and college but started one of New York City's largest real estate companies. She is also an investor and stars on ABC's *Shark Tank*. Mary Callahan was the first woman to major in mathematics from Georgetown University, worked as a mailroom clerk at a bank and built her way up. She is now one of the most powerful women in finance and might succeed Jamie Dimon as CEO of JP Morgan. These women have inspired me and given me hope that women can be successful leaders in industries that are male dominated."

Early Years

Michelle Sindhunirmala graduated from New York University (NYU) in 2019 with a BS in Hotel Management and a concentration in real estate. Michelle figured out that she wanted to pursue finance in the second semester of her sophomore year. However, it was too late to make her class credits accommodate the change to a different major.

In her sophomore year of college, Michelle worked as a waitress at a Michelin star restaurant in New York, quickly realizing that the job was not as intellectually thrilling as she wanted it to be. She did a lot of research on how to start a career in, and interview for, investment banking and asset management. When she started looking for jobs, she realized how difficult it was to jump right into finance: "It is so frustrating. You have to network more than once a week. You apply for one hundred jobs, hear back from sixty, and probably get an offer from two." She turned to real estate as a good transition from hotel management to finance. In 2017, she landed three internships in that sector and one in asset management.

After many friends and colleagues encouraged her to try investment banking, Michelle successfully applied for an internship as an investment banking summer analyst at Raymond James. When the internship ended, Michelle walked away with two things: a full-time job offer from the company and the realization that she did not enjoy investment banking. She ended up turning down the job offer.

Path to Success

Michelle looks forward to pursuing a career in asset management or portfolio management in technology, consumer goods, retail, or real estate. As of March 2020, she works as a real estate valuation and advisory analyst with a focus on global accounts at Altus Group, a commercial real estate company based in Canada

Philosophy

In college, Michelle was a part of all-women's investment groups that helped her feel supported in a male-dominated environment. She received two pieces of advice that she carries with her: 1) "Drill down on all the questions you have. Speak up, and don't be afraid to ask for help";

and 2) "You're a woman. What can you do? Show them what you're capable of, perform well, and try your best."

My Story

Transcript of Maya Peterson's Talk at the Markel Corporation's Jitney Group in January 2019
Investing - Experience Versus Knowledge

Experience and knowledge are the two key elements of investing. There are countless ways for aspiring investors to gain knowledge whether it is through books or online sources. Making your brain sweat is great, but nothing can replace experience. Reading about workout routines and a TRX system is really not the same thing as going to the gym. The same principle applies to investing; there is no way to really understand investing until you just do it.

The first being the importance of experience. There is a common saying: "Buy low. Sell high." That makes sense, right? But to buy low means that it is only when the market drops, your palms get sweaty, you feel unsure, you look at your stock quote, and it is in that bright red color, do you understand that saying. It is one thing to read "Buy low. Sell high" in a book. Of course, it makes logical sense when you read it, but it is quite another thing to actually do it.

I am not an emotional investor. I research all the stocks I buy; I do not go off of other people's opinions. I do my own research to find companies that meet my criteria. Although I am not an emotional investor, I am still a human, and when I look at my quarterly reports and know that only a small fraction of my holdings went up, I do get a certain unhappy feeling. But as long as I am still confident in the businesses, I resist the urge to sell.

Investing is about making sure that after I work and save my money, my money will work for me. When I take the money, I have saved from jobs and choose to invest it, I am becoming a part-owner of a business. A tiny, little slice, regardless of how much I own, I am still a "part-owner of the business," so I have to make sure I understand what that business does, who runs it, and how they stand up to the competition. If I understand that, then the investment should work out fine over the long haul.

My experiences have helped to reinforce the importance of a disciplined approach to investing. After seven years of learning from the mistakes I have made, I work harder to try to answer the questions about the business. Of course, it is not foolproof, and I have made mistakes along the way. My first holding was my worst mistake and my best experience. When I was nine years old, I sold my American Girl dolls. I used that money to buy my first shares of a company, Mattel, which makes American Girl Dolls, as well as Barbie, Hot Wheels, and more.

I knew a bunch about Mattel's products, but as it played out, I learned that my experience was far from my knowledge. I focused on the products of Mattel because I loved playing with them. Because I am a math nerd, I checked my work by running the numbers of Mattel. I knew that they had a satisfactory dividend, an acceptable Return on Equity, impressive profit margins, low debt, and a reasonable Price/Earnings ratio. I was feeling confident in my choice. Since this was my first investment, I assumed that all the checkboxes next to each of the metrics on my index card plus all my firsthand knowledge of dolls and toys meant that I was all good to become a Mattel shareholder. However, my experience was quite different, over the next couple of years, Mattel's shares went down and down, 30% down, 40% down, and further down into the red numbers.

So, what happened? I learned that investing is not just products and numbers, rather you are a part-owner of a business, and businesses only exist in marketplaces, and marketplaces are always changing. Plus, competitors come at you from places you do not expect. In the case of Mattel seven years ago, the iPhone was still new, Amazon was big, but not as big as it is now, iPads were barely getting started, and last but not least, the movie "Frozen" had not been released yet. Sometimes you just have to let go and learn from events. What did my products and numbers analysis miss? I was unaware of how stores closing like Toys R Us impacted Mattel's earnings when the sustainability of Toys R Us business started to wane from the negative impact of iPhones and other devices on the demand for children's toys, Mattel was soon in a world of hurt. I knew their products and their numbers which, for a nine-year-old, was not bad at all, but I did not figure on the iPhone. Why do I call an investment where I am down about 35% on paper one of my best? Simple, the experience I gained from my Mattel investment is to try to know that the story of the company and the market it operates in was just as important as the product and numbers.

The second thing I learned from my Mattel experience is humility. My shares of Mattel fell below their price during the Great Recession. I was wrong, but I have continued to invest in other companies, working not to repeat my mistakes, and become a part-owner in many businesses, because as Edmund Burke said, "Nobody made a greater mistake than he who did nothing because he could do only a little." Becoming a shareholder of Mattel was the worst best thing that ever happened to me because that experience helped me connect many dots, I would have otherwise struggled to draw a line between.

If you are a fan of detective stories like me, then you probably know Father Brown by GK Chesterton. I did not know this quote at the time I invested in Mattel, but it is a good way to think about it:

> *"The real trouble with this world of ours is not that it is an unreasonable world, nor even that it is a reasonable one. The commonest kind of trouble is that it is nearly reasonable, but not quite... It looks just a little more mathematical and regular than it is; its exactitude is obvious, but its inexactitude is hidden; its wildness lies in wait."*

Humility really matters in investing, investing is about the future, and the future is unpredictable. Staying humble means understanding that no matter how hard you crunch the numbers, this isn't a calculus class, and the answer you derive is never perfect. One day, it is kids playing with dolls, and the next day some California guy in a black turtleneck puts a piece of metal in everyone's hands, and a 60-year-old toymaker goes poof. Not even math can protect you then. Numbers can sometimes tell you if you are wrong, but by themselves, numbers are not enough to be right. In the end, it is all about moats.

Investing has also taught me to work hard on analysis. I like to call it nerdiness. Making mistakes is part of the process, it happens to everyone. But not everyone learns from their mistakes. Wouldn't you rather learn how I lost money on Mattel and know not to make that same mistake yourself? Nerdiness allows you to keep your mind open to new information and have an ongoing desire to learn from others.

Every year since I was nine, I attended the Markel Insurance annual shareholders' meeting in Omaha, Nebraska. Since I was already in Omaha, I also like to stop in at Berkshire Hathaway's annual meeting too. Both events are packed with investors from all over the world coming to learn what they can learn from Warren Buffett and Tom Gayner over one weekend in May. Knowledge is not only formed from reading "Intelligent Investor" by Benjamin Graham but from learning directly from others' experience.

About four years ago, I met another investor who had a big influence on me, an 89-year-old woman who had a passion for numbers. Her name is Ginny. Our meeting to discuss her story and her holdings started with the tough decision of deciding what type of tea we wanted. The conversation quickly transitioned to scones and then to investing. Ginny's house is in a tiny town in northern Minnesota, not far from Canada, and nowhere near Manhattan. She was not wearing a three-piece suit barking demands at her assistant. She was sitting around her kitchen table looking out at the lake. Ginny wore a smart blue sweater and sat at her table with the spreadsheets, annual reports, and countless newspapers covering the companies she was a part-owner in. Ginny's first stock was given to her as a wedding gift in the 1940s from her father in law. His gift inspired a lifelong passion for investing for Ginny.

Her investing style is simple: She finds simple to understand businesses- nothing fancy, the companies that make household products like paint or the products in your kitchen or medicine cabinet. From there, she looks at the numbers and watches the people. How she invests has been a major influence on how I invest.

After meeting Ginny, it was very clear to me how little flash there was in investing, and I learned the importance of having a frugal mindset. Since I was young, I have never enjoyed spending my money. I enjoy making money and then investing it, but it pains me to take a dollar out of my wallet and spend it on something I want. When I earn money, my first thought is not how much to spend, it is how much and where to invest it. If I made a list of all the things I would rather do than spend my money, first on the list would be to invest it.

Bankrate data says that, currently, less than 57% of Americans have $1,000 in savings.[14] That is scary, but what is worse is that I know my teenage friends have significantly less than that and spend almost all of their money on daily trips to the vending machine. I will admit that I can relate to the appeal of Pepsi. I own a few shares. Vending machine products are designed to be cheap. What will a bag of $1 chips do to your future? You're right in thinking nothing. One dollar will do nothing to your future unless you choose to save it. If I were to spend $2.25 on a bag of M&Ms and a bag of Skittles every day for 165 days, which is approximately a whole school year, my midday snacks would total to $371.25. To me, that's a lot of money. If my trips to the vending machine continued every school day for four years of high school, I would have spent $1,485 on candy by the last day of my senior year.

What if I decided to invest the money that I otherwise would've spent on candy with a 10% annual interest rate? If I invested it from the first day in freshman year of high school to my last day in college, my money would have doubled. If I kept investing $1,485 until I retired, about 45 years after high school, I would have over $100,000. The day I did that math my vending machine budget began to resemble a donut.

My spewing out numbers about what your life could look like if you made different choices sounds similar to getting rich quick; however, investing could not be more long term. A lot of it is little things plus discipline, held over a long-time frame. Here is a simple example, let's say you are not going to retire for about 20-30 years. You can look at a purchase you are considering and multiply it by 15. If you are young enough or not going to retire for 20-30 years, then a dollar could easily be worth 15 times more with that long time to compound. So, then when you see that new $300 golf club or whatever else might interest you in that second, think of it not as a $300 purchase, but rather losing out on $4,500 in retirement. Now, if you are able to invest that money in a successful company such as Markel, then you might do even better. The simple lesson here is to multiply optional purchases by 15, or less if you are older or want to be more conservative and try to get another year or two out of those old golf clubs.

Not buying your $300 golf clubs the day you want them takes discipline. The discipline in saving is just as important in investing. It is quite easy to urge people to buy low and sell high, but when the time comes, it becomes harder, no matter how many times you've repeated this precept to friends, family, bosses, coworkers, everyone. Investing teaches you a collection of things. Investing has allowed me to see the world differently.

As an investor, I feel like a greater, more influential force in the world. Most teenagers cannot drive themselves around, but they can choose to save and invest. If you think about it, investing can be the first adult choice you get to make. It is a really powerful decision to save your money and choose to buy into certain companies. Little things that I otherwise would not pay attention to, such as if my friends still buy Tiffany jewelry or wear Nike shoes, become critically important to me because investing in the soda your brother is drinking, could allow you to have financial independence early on in your life.

As a business owner, I like to own companies that make money. One area I like to invest in is consumer staples. I don't look out for the next cryptocurrency hot stock or how marijuana is doing. Instead, I monitor shampoo and paper towels. I find that significantly more interesting because when you own companies that make things that people buy at Walmart every day, it makes it easy to monitor how the companies are doing and if they are growing or not. If someone consistently uses Dove soap, Crest toothpaste, or any other day to day product, it is a pretty safe bet that the consumer's habits will not change over very long timeframes.

The world of business owners is filled with interesting stories. Here is one more, Rose Blumkin, who was known as Mrs. B. She founded Nebraska Furniture Mart in 1937. Berkshire Hathaway acquired the company in 1983, making Mrs. B the first female manager at Berkshire.

Before Nebraska Furniture Mart, Mrs. B was a Russian immigrant with a mind made for business. She learned the ways of business from her mother, and at age thirteen Mrs. B walked 18 miles to another city in Russia to find a well-paying job out of town to support her family. She was persistent and stubborn even as a child.

When the war started, she had no other option but to flee Russia. She said, "I had no passport. At the China-Russia frontier, a soldier was standing guard with a rifle. I said to him, 'I am on the way to buy leather for the Army. When I come back, I'll bring you a big bottle of vodka.' I suppose he's still waiting there for his vodka."

Isadore Blumkin, her husband, opened a small second-hand clothing store that made around $10 per week. He sold his clothing at the same price he bought them for, making no profit. This was far from ideal during the depression. Mrs. B was quick to correct him, "You buy a pair of shoes for $3, sell them for $3.30." Mrs. B had built a large business for her boss back in Russia, and she knew she could do the same here in America. Isadore's income was not enough, so she started her own business that year in the basement of her husband's pawn shop with $500 her brother loaned to her. She learned the best way to have returning customers is to make a small profit of 10% and do anything for them. She didn't believe that success and power were made because of cheating someone out of their dollar or scaring them into a purchase.

Customers loved her prices, but certain suppliers felt differently. Mrs. B said, "The merchants were very rotten to me. When I walked into Merchandise Mart to buy furniture, to buy anything, they used to kick me out and say, 'Don't bother us. We're not going to sell you nothing.' I used to almost start to cry. My face would get red and I'd say, 'Someday you'll come to my store to try to sell to me, and I'll kick you out the same way that you did to me.'"

There was no competition with her low prices, and even at age 100, she worked 12-14 hours a day, 7 days a week.

To be a successful investor, I feel as if a little part of Mrs. B has to exist in you. She was focused on her customers and took every challenge she faced head on knowing that in the long term her customers' loyalty would make a profitable business. Mrs. B was rich with experience and an entrepreneurial spirit that could never be outshined.

One of the best parts of writing my first book, *Early Bird: The Power of Investing Young*, was to see what other people did with it, it became a tool for discussions in hundreds of families. Last year I talked with two motivating and eye-opening people named Barbara and Bob, who want to try and inspire their grandchildren towards the long term focused investing path. When my book came out, they purchased a copy for each of their nine grandchildren, with ages ranging from 12 to 20 years old.

On Christmas, all the grandchildren opened their presents to see a copy of *Early Bird* and a contract from their grandparents. The contract stated that the grandchildren had to read *Early Bird* and use the ideas in there to pick a stock to invest in. As long as they followed up and ran the analysis on the stocks, the grandparents would give them money every year for five years for investing purposes only. The deal was sealed when the grandchild sent a signed contract back confirming their investment choice, proof of perusal of *Early Bird*, and commitment to the challenge their grandparents call "The Investment Challenge."

I'm proud to say my book was a gift to many people across generations, but this is by far the best plan I have seen to add more incentive and discipline for early birds to invest and get started. It is a great feeling to think of the thousands of people who have bought the book, how many new investors and investing accounts have been created out of the book. Investing is a learning process, and I enjoy thinking about the conversations people have had and what they learn on their own investing journey. Just in Barbara and Bob's family alone, there are nine new accounts compounding away for the grandkids. The family recently wrote and reported they completed their second year of funding accounts for their Early Bird challenge after achieving roughly 8% gains in 2018.

I was interviewed for a newspaper when my book was originally published, and the article was well researched and written, but one quotation about why I invested in Pepsi will forever haunt me. According to the reporter, I said, "I picked Pepsi because I love Sun Chips. Cheddar Sun Chips are my favorite — that's how I pick most of my stocks."

The reporter left out a major part of the process. First, I watch what new things my friends bring into school, make careful observations about products used in the world, and find products I like, like Sun Chips. After that, I look to see if the company has a stable competitive moat that I predict will work out for the long term. Next, I try to learn as much as I can about the company. I make sure the numbers back up the story and then wait for the company to get to my desired price. Buying a stock is just the start because businesses are always changing, and so once I buy, I monitor how my companies are doing in the marketplace.

I would buy many bags of Sun Chips because I like the product, but I would not buy even one share of a company just because I like their product. Investing should be as simple as possible, but buying a stock takes more work than just eating Sun Chips.

Over these past seven years, I have developed an investing mindset of patience, frugality, nerdiness, humility, and discipline. To put in the work to build your knowledge of the business and then to monitor progress so you can learn from real experience. The best way to learn to invest is to just invest. Investing is simple to understand: You put in your work, try to understand the business, and do your best to pick stocks; however, the world is unpredictable, and things do not always go as planned. Through investing I have learned to look at the world differently. The world of business becomes much clearer when you are a business focused investor.

The simple act of understanding business has the ability to benefit anyone just by building your knowledge. When you have the experience of being an engaged part owner, it adds another tool in your toolbox. Because as a business owner, you need to continually review the strength of your competitive moat against the marketplace. It is an ongoing process of checking and rechecking your work. I hope my stories have helped inspire someone to start investing in their future because all it takes "is wet snow and a really long hill."

Appendix A

SRI and ESG

The lighthouses in this book are women making real change today that set the world up for even more tomorrow. They are ahead of the curve. According to many professionals I spoke to, socially responsible investing (SRI) and environmental, social, and governance (ESG) investing are among the most popular investing movements of the last decade. Some of the women discussed in this book were SRI and ESG champions in the field long before it was popular to advocate for social responsibility. With more interest in the field, new options emerge.

Social responsibility means that individuals and corporations have a civic duty to benefit society, or at least not harm it. If corporate social responsibility (CSR) is about making a "greener" impact on the environment, creating a diverse and open-minded workforce, and/or benefiting society over the long term, why is it so hard for companies to do? The short answer is: the long term. People and companies too often focus on the short term: how much money their company will make this quarter. If their drive is making money in the short term, then, as British asset management guru Jeremy Grantham said at the 2018 Morningstar investment conference in Chicago, "Grandchildren have no value ... We deforest the land, we degrade our soils, we pollute and overuse our water, and we treat our air like an open sewer. All of this is off the balance sheet and off the income statement."

For a socially responsible investor, the money a company will make next quarter is insignificant relative to the company's social and environmental impact twenty years from now. *How* the company makes its profits is crucial. Both value investing *and* social responsibility require a long-term mindset. If investors don't change their mindset, making corporations socially responsible will be a long-term *problem*. Although your grandchildren might not be your main concern when you are reviewing your second-quarter profits, think about a time when supply cannot match the demand of the population. I am not talking about a supply of new Adidas shoes, but about that future time when the resources necessary for life are no longer available. By investing in companies that will do *whatever* it takes to make an extra dollar *now,* you, as an investor, are helping to confirm this grim future. Only when investors value corporate social responsibility just as much as they do dividends will there be a change in the environmental and social aspects of businesses (see Figure 2 below).[15]

Figure 2. Incremental Renewable Additions and Investment Size

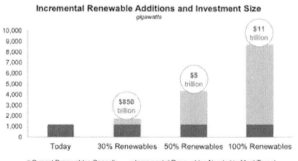

Investors have the opportunity to be leaders in the field of social responsibility—for example, by investing trillions of dollars in companies that deliver renewable energy. The answer is not in companies that greenwash consumers. It is in the hands of the investors. It is their choice as to where to put their money.

Below is Alyce Lomax and John Rotonti's published ESG Investing Framework referenced in Alyce Lomax's chapter in this book.[16] It is a checklist to filter companies that score a seven or better. This framework shows how long-term investing and long-term thinking line up for investors looking for companies that can excel over the long haul:

1. Does the company treat its employees well?

2. Is the company a good steward of the environment?

3. Does the company promote diversity and inclusion?

4. Does the company have ethical corporate governance principles?

5. Do the company's business model and its investments promote ESG principles?

6. Does the company have a healthy balance sheet?

7. Can the company generate organic revenue growth supported by long-term tailwinds?

8. Can the business generate growing FCF and sustain high ROIC?

9. Is the management team focused on driving long-term profitable growth?

10. Does the company have a medium- or lower-risk profile?

Throughout her searches, Alyce Lomax found Starbucks to be an incredible example of corporate social responsibility. Starbucks became one of the first companies to provide health benefits, shares of stock, and free college tuition programs to full- and part-time employees. "[There is a great need] to achieve the fragile balance between profit, social impact, and a moral obligation ... to enhance the lives of our employees and the communities we serve," says Howard Schultz, executive chairman of Starbucks.[17] Starbucks has supported 227 college graduates with tuition-free education through its Starbucks College Achievement Plan.[18]

Starbucks is socially responsible in two main ways: through its employees and products. Its coffee is 99 percent ethically sourced, and the company has invested $50 million in funding for farmers to provide 100 million coffee plants to their one million coffee farmers by 2025.[19] Starbucks carefully purchases each ingredient to make sure the source is ethical. The company donates money to provide farmers with disease-resistant coffee plants and raises money to pay farmers to make their farms more sustainable. By 2020, Starbucks hopes to have its tea and cocoa 100 percent ethically sourced.[20]

Starbucks also invests in building communities. The company undertakes a range of actions to enhance the community, such as launching a full-ride scholarship at Arizona State University, donating money to its farmers to help improve their lives and to local companies in Seattle (the company's hometown), and providing opportunities for youth interaction with the world and community service.[21] Starbucks wants to reduce its environmental footprint and is building stores with energy conservation, using resources that are good for the environment, and ensuring that all its cups are recyclable. Starbucks estimated that its stores disposed of 8,070,428 cups per day. That means that in the thirty-six years of Starbucks's existence something like 1,060,454,239,000 cups were trashed![22] Now that they recycle all of their cups, few go to waste.

Alyce's other example, Costco, is also socially responsible, mainly with its employees. Costco does not force corporate social responsibility.[23] The average employee is paid $21 per hour, and 88 percent of the employees have sponsored health and dental care.[24] Even during the 2007–2009 recession, Costco raised hourly wages by $1.50 over those three years. The company's sustainability over the long term is due to making working conditions comfortable for the employees. Costco has a 94 percent employee retention rate. Seventy percent of the warehouse managers started at the cash register, which employees view as a sign of a promising future at the company. Walmart's CEO is paid 782 times the average Walmart employee's wage, whereas Costco's CEO's salary is forty-eight times the average Costco employee's wage.[25]

Appendix B

Telephone Interview Dates

Katherine Fischer	July 18, 2019
Shilpa Andalkar	July 18, 2019
Heather Brilliant	July 19, 2019
Lauren Templeton	July 19, 2019
Monsoon Pabrai	July 20, 2019
Erin Lash	July 22, 2019
Lisa Shalett	July 23, 2019
Perth Tolle	July 23, 2019
Fran Skinner	July 24, 2019
Sonya Dreizler	July 24, 2019
Denise Strack	August 5, 2019
Michelle Sindhunirmala	August 5, 2019
Lisa Tepper	August 30, 2019
Vicki Saunders	September 7, 2019
Alyce Lomax	November 3, 2019
Margaret Rust	November 14, 2019
Callie Haines	November 18, 2019
Jenn Cole	February 18, 2020
Jen Likander	February 26, 2020

Glossary

BRICs: Acronym for the five major developing countries of Brazil, Russia, Indian, China, and South America.

Certified financial analyst (CFA): Professional certification for financial professions such as portfolio management and investment analysis.

Certified financial planner (CFP): Professional qualification for financial planning.

Certified public accountant (CPA): License allowing certified professionals to offer accounting services to the public.

C-suite: Group of chief executives within an organization.

Exchange-traded fund (ETF): Fund comprised of assets such as bonds, stocks, and commodities traded on stock exchanges.

Free cash flow (FCF): Cash remaining in a company after paying operating expenses and capital expenditures.

Flat company: Company striving to be nonhierarchical and interdisciplinary.

Index fund: Type of mutual fund or ETF.

Issuer: Legal individual or organization developing, registering, and selling financial securities.

Financial moat: Competitive advantages of a given company

Return on invested capital (ROIC): Measurement of profitability determined by the net operating profit and total invested capital.

Ticker symbol: Letters representing a specific security.

Sources

[1] Fortune Editors, "Female CFOs in the Fortune 500," Fortune magazine, February 24, 2015, https://fortune.com/2015/02/24/female-cfos-fortune-500/.

[2] Alexis Krivkovich, Kelsey Robinson, Irina Starikova, Rachel Valentino, and Lareina Yee, "Women in the Workplace 2017," McKinsey & Company, accessed December 24, 2019, https://www.mckinsey.com/featured-insights/gender-equality/women-in-the-workplace-2017.

[3] W. Brad Johnson and David G. Smith, "How Men Can Become Better Allies to Women," *Harvard Business Review*, October 12, 2018, https://hbr.org/2018/10/how-men-can-become-better-allies-to-women.

[4] Jessica Bennett, "Do Women-Only Networking Groups Help or Hurt Female Entrepreneurs?" *Inc.* magazine, accessed December 26, 2019, https://www.inc.com/magazine/201710/jessica-bennett/women-coworking-spaces.html.

[5] Light, Paulette. "Why 43% of Women with Children Leave Their Jobs, and How to Get Them Back." *The Atlantic,* April 19, 2013, accessed December 26, 2019, https://www.theatlantic.com/sexes/archive/2013/04/why-43-of-women-

with-children-leave-their-jobs-and-how-to-get-them-back/275134/

[6] Jeremy Grantham. "The Race of Our Lives Revisited," Morningstar, June 25, 2018, https://www.morningstar.com/articles/870606/watch-jeremy-granthams-race-of-our-lives-speech.

[7] See "Warren Buffett, Quotes" at Goodreads, https://www.goodreads.com/quotes/117851-life-is-like-a-snowball-the-important-thing-is-finding.

[8] "Freedom 100 Emerging Markets Index." Life + Liberty Indexes. https://www.lifeandlibertyindexes.com/freedom-100-emerging-markets-index (accessed on December 31st, 2019).

[9] Frances Denmark, "Denise Strack Has Endowment Management Down to a Science," Institutional Investor, May 10, 2016, accessed November 13, 2019, https://www.institutionalinvestor.com/article/b14z9qccwxvlzy/denise-strack-has-endowment-management-down-to-a-science.

[10] Kimberly Amadeo, "Consumer Spending Statistics and Current Trends," The Balance, updated February 6, 2020, accessed on February 24, 2020, https://www.thebalance.com/consumer-spending-trends-and-current-statistics-3305916.

[11] Markel, "The Markel Style," accessed on February 29, 2020, https://www.markel.com/about-markel/markel-style.

[12] Ibid.

[13] Mohr, Tara Sophia, "Why Women Don't Apply for Jobs Unless They're 100% Qualified," *Harvard Business Review*, August 25, 2014, accessed on October 3, 2019, https://hbr.org/2014/08/why-women-dont-apply-for-jobs-unless-theyre-100-qualified.

[14] Martin, Emmie, "Few Americans have Enough Savings to Cover a $1000 Emergency," January 18, 2018, https://www.cnbc.com/2018/01/18/few-americans-have-enough-savings-to-cover-a-1000-emergency.html

[15] "Brookfield Renewable Partners: Corporate Profile," November, 2019, https://bep.brookfield.com/~/media/Files/B/Brookfield-BEP-IR-V2/events-and-presentations/bep-corporate-profile-november-2019-vf2.pdf.

[16] Lomax, Alyce. John Rotonti. "Going for Great Returns and the Greater Good: The Motley Fool's ESG Investing Framework," The Motley Fool, April 9, 2019, https://www.fool.com/investing/2019/04/09/going-for-great-returns-and-the-greater-good-fools.aspx

[17] Tanya Mohn, "Howard Schultz, Starbucks and a History of Corporate Responsibility," *New York Times*, November 15, 2017, accessed on October 10, 2018, https://www.nytimes.com/2017/11/15/business/dealbook/howard-schultz-starbucks-corporate-responsibility.html.

[18] Ibid.

[19] Starbucks, "Starbucks Social Impact, accessed October 10, 2018, https://www.starbucks.com/responsibility.

[20] Ibid.

[21] Ibid.

[22] Ibid.

[23] Costco Wholesale Corporation, "Sustainability Commitment, 2019 Update," https://www.costco.com/sustainability-introduction.html.

[24] Michael Tsangaris, "Investing the Socially Responsible Way," The Motley Fool, December 31, 2013, October 10, 2018, https://www.fool.com/investing/general/2013/12/31/investing-the-socially-responsible-way.aspx.

[25] Costco Wholesale Corporation, "Sustainability Commitment, 2019 Update," https://www.costco.com/sustainability-introduction.html.

Made in the USA
Monee, IL
09 May 2020